Painting
Techniques
&FAUX FINISHES

Painting Techniques

& FAUX FINISHES

By Louise Hennigs and Marina Niven

Photography by Craig Fraser & Deidi von Schaewen

CREATIVE PUBLISHING international

First published in the USA and Canada in 1998 by Creative Publishing international, Inc.

5900 Green Oak Drive
Minnetonka, Minnesota 55343
1-800-328-3895

Edited by Hilda Hermann
Photography by Craig Fraser & Deidi von Schaewen
Design by Petal Palmer
Reproduction by Hirt & Carter (Pty) Cape Town
Printed and bound in Singapore by Tien Wah Press

ISBN 0-86573-182-9

contents

Acknowledgments

Our special thanks go to Nella Opperman and Charlotte Wright for their inspiration and encouragement, and for teaching us all we know about decorative paint finishes; to photographers Craig Fraser and Deidi von Schaewen for their magnificent photographs; to designer Petal Palmer for her enthusiasm while photographing this book; and to Peter Sullivan and Marilyn Brain for allowing us to photograph their lovely homes.

INTRODUCTION

Paint has always had a dual role as a practical, protective covering and as an important form of creative expression. Throughout history, there has been a universal need to decorate dwellings and places of worship. During the Renaissance, artists were commissioned by royalty and wealthy patrons to adorn their palaces with lavish imagery and colors. These artists are regarded as the originators of the popular decorative painting techniques that are pursued today.

Paint is one of the most simple and effective ways of transforming interiors, exteriors and furniture, and can be used to create a seemingly endless variety of decorative finishes.

The chapter on materials and equipment will introduce you to the different paints, glazes, varnishes and equipment needed for the decorative paint finishes described in this book. Guidelines are given for the correct preparation of working surfaces for walls, woodwork, floors, metalwork, plastics and ceramics. Color is one of the most important aspects to consider when decorating with any paint finish and the basics of color theory and color mixing are reviewed in the section on color.

Among the basic techniques for you to try are color washing and rubbing, dragging, flogging, ragging, spattering, sponging and stippling. Don't be afraid of making mistakes and remember to enjoy yourself! There is very little that a coat of paint cannot fix and, if necessary, you can always start again. Faux lacquer, lapis lazuli, malachite, marbling, shagreen, stone blocking and tortoiseshell are the more challenging techniques to master. The section on aging and antiquing will provide you with the tricks of the trade to make virtually anything look old. All the techniques are illustrated with step-by-step photographs and easy-to-follow instructions.

We hope that this book will encourage and inspire both curious newcomers and more experienced decorators to master the basic techniques and to experiment with paint effects.

LOUISE HENNIGS & MARINA NIVEN

introduction

materials
and equipment

THIS CHAPTER INTRODUCES YOU TO THE DIFFERENT PAINTS, GLAZES,

VARNISHES AND EQUIPMENT NEEDED FOR THE DECORATIVE PAINT FINISHES

DESCRIBED IN THE BOOK. MOST ITEMS CAN BE FOUND AT YOUR LOCAL

PAINT DEALER OR ART STORE, ALTHOUGH SOME OF THE FINISHING

BRUSHES AND TOOLS MAY HAVE TO BE PURCHASED AT STORES

SPECIALIZING IN DECORATIVE SUPPLIES. WHEN CHOOSING EQUIPMENT

AND MATERIALS, USE THE BEST PRODUCTS THAT YOU CAN. THE BETTER THE

TOOLS, THE EASIER IT WILL BE TO MASTER THE TECHNIQUE.

*Careful and thorough
preparation is the key to success
with paint techniques.*

PAINT

WITH TODAY'S ADVANCED TECHNOLOGY, PAINT MANUFACTURERS PRODUCE SO MANY DIFFERENT TYPES OF PAINT THAT CHOOSING THE RIGHT ONE FOR A PARTICULAR TASK CAN BE DAUNTING. IT HELPS TO HAVE A BASIC UNDERSTANDING OF PAINT, ITS COMPOSITION AND ITS USES WHEN CONFRONTED WITH THE VARIETIES AVAILABLE.

ALL PAINTS ARE MADE UP OF A *PIGMENT* WHICH PROVIDES COLOR, A *BINDER* OR MEDIUM IN WHICH THE PIGMENT IS SUSPENDED AND WHICH BINDS THE PAINT TO THE SURFACE, AND A *SOLVENT* WHICH DILUTES THE MIXTURE TO MAKE IT FLOW SMOOTHLY AND EVENLY. THE SOLVENT EVAPORATES IN THE DRYING PROCESS AND LEAVES AN EVEN, DRY COATING ON THE SURFACE. THE DURABILITY, HARDNESS AND ABSORBENCY OF THE PAINTED SURFACE DEPENDS ON THE TYPE OF PIGMENT, BINDER AND SOLVENT USED.

TYPES OF WATER-BASED PAINT

Alternative names	latex, emulsion, vinyl emulsion, polyvinylacrylic (PVA)
Pigment	synthetic or natural powder color
Binder	acrylic resin
Solvent	water

When preparing to mix paints make sure that you have enough suitable containers, plates or small dishes in which to mix the paints, solvents and glazes. It is also useful to keep a supply of latex surgical gloves available to use when you are doing messy techniques.

Water-based house paint

In the past, houses were painted both inside and out with a paint called whitewash or distemper. This was a simple mixture of lime or chalk, hide glue or size, and water. Alternatively, limestone was soaked in water, which naturally heated to a boiling mass, and animal fat was added to it as a binder. The mixture was allowed to subside and ferment until it was ready to use. Natural pigments like ochre or red oxide could be added to give it color.

Today, the natural ingredients have been replaced with synthetic substitutes, making the paints more durable and easier to use. They are available in different finishes, ranging from flat/matte to midsheen/eggshell/satin. Some paint manufacturers have produced high-gloss, water-based paint.

All water-based paints can be diluted with water, and any equipment used should be cleaned with water. Once a water-based paint has dried, it is no longer water soluble.

Artists' acrylic paint

These are tubes of water-soluble paint that can be used either on their own for small-scale artwork on furniture, or as colorants in water-based paint. They can also be diluted with water and used as a color wash.

A students' acrylic is also available, and is usually cheaper than artists' acrylic, but not as good quality. There are many other types of water-based artists' paint, but they are unsuitable for the techniques in this book.

Water-based glaze

Water-based glaze (sometimes called acrylic scumble glaze) is a fairly recent addition to the list of decorative painting materials and, in some cases, can be used as a substitute for oil glaze. Often called acrylic medium, it is a transparent gel-like substance that appears milky when wet, but dries to a clear finish. It can be colored and is diluted with water. This type of glaze retards the drying process of water-based paints, giving one more time to create decorative finishes.

Water-based varnish

Water-based varnish is a very useful medium as it is quick drying and durable. It is suitable for protecting all water-based paint finishes and is available in a flat/matte or midsheen/suede finish.

It is a milky color when wet, but dries completely clear when applied over the surface in a thin, even layer.

If it is applied too thickly, it will appear cloudy when dry. This varnish does not discolor with age, which has made it more popular than oil-based varnishes.

TYPES OF OIL-BASED PAINT	
Alternative names	alkyd, enamel
Pigment	synthetic or natural powder color
Binder	synthetic resin or drying oil
Solvent	mineral spirits

Oil-based paint

Oil-based paint is hard-wearing and used for interior walls in high-traffic areas and for protecting interior and exterior woodwork. In the past there was only one type of oil paint, but it is now available in flat/matte, mid-sheen/semi-gloss/satin/eggshell and gloss.

Some manufacturers have produced a variety of sheens with modifications for easier application, quicker drying time, or non-drip, non-stir thixotropic (gel-based) paint.

It is always advisable to ask your paint supplier to recommend the correct type of paint for a specific purpose.

Artists' oils

These are primarily used for painting on canvas, but are an excellent source of pure color for tinting oil-based paints and glazes. They are also available in a students' quality at a cheaper price, but the colors are not as saturated or as strong as the artists' quality. Artists' oils can be extended with linseed oil and diluted with mineral spirits.

Paint manufacturers produce a contractors' quality and a more superior quality paint. The difference is often noticeable in the price (contractors' quality being cheaper) and the paint's durability. Some cheaper water-based paints are dry, dull and chalky and often too absorbent for decorative paint finishes. However, some are of such superior quality that they dry as strong as any oil-based paint and can be used as a base for oil-based decorative techniques.

materials and equipment

Oil-based varnish

Oil-based varnish is a protective coating used on painted surfaces and woodwork. Polyurethane varnish is the most commonly used all-purpose varnish, and is available in flat/matte, semi-sheen/suede or gloss. It is yellow and darkens with age, which must be taken into consideration when it is used to protect a colored surface – for example, a pale blue decorative finish could discolor to green with age. It can be colored with artists' oils. There are many types of oil-based varnish, such as yacht varnish, which is very dark and weather resistant, and a variety of wood-stain varnishes.

Oil-based glaze

Often referred to as scumble glaze, this is a transparent medium used over a base coat of oil-based paint to create decorative finishes. It can be colored with diluted artists' oils or universal stainers. Scumble glaze is a creamy color and thick before it is mixed to the required strength. It dries quite transparent, allowing the base color to show through, which makes it suitable for a variety of decorative finishes, woodgraining and faux marbling. When it is mixed according to a formula, it flows easily and can hold a pattern or mark without dripping. Scumble glaze cannot be used on its own as a paint or varnish as it has no inherent properties. It must always be mixed with an oil-based paint (artists' oils for transparent color; alkyd for opaque color) and mineral spirits in equal parts (1:1:1).

STORING PAINT

When you are finished painting, make sure the can's rim and the edge of the lid are free of paint. Press the lid down and give it a few knocks with a hammer to secure it. This will keep air out and stop a skin from forming on the paint's surface.

Store paint, glaze and varnish away from direct sunlight or heat. Make sure all the containers are labeled with their contents and where they were used, so that you can find them easily.

If paint forms a skin on the surface, remove the skin and strain the remaining paint through an old stocking to remove any lumps.

OTHER MATERIALS
Whiting (calcium carbonate)

This is a white pigment used to color water-based and oil-based paints. Transparent bases do not contain whiting. It is also used to stop beading when a water-based finish is applied to an oil-based surface.

Rottenstone

Rottenstone is a fine, light brown powder which is used as a mild abrasive to give texture to some antiquing techniques.

Vinegar

Household apple cider vinegar is used in some water-based finishes to make the paint sticky so that it will adhere to an oil-based surface.

Shellac

Shellac is a varnish made from the sticky resin of the lac beetle. It is normally dark brown in color, but is also available in a range of orange colors and bleached clear. In its dry state, it comes in flake form or as little beads called seedlac. It dissolves in denatured alcohol to become a soft varnish. It is also used to seal the knots in raw wood.

Denatured alcohol/methylated spirits

These solvents, used to dissolve shellac and to clean off dried latex paint, are also used in some solvent-release techniques. Methyl violet is added to ethyl alcohol to make it poisonous and undrinkable.

Benzine/naphtha

This is a petroleum-distillate solvent used in solvent-release techniques.

Powder pigments

Ground-up pigments give a very pure color and are often used to make paint. Earth-colored pigments are sometimes used in antiquing.

BRUSHES

Brushes are manufactured in a range of sizes, shapes and qualities, and have various uses. The most commonly found brushes are those used for household painting and varnishing. Artists' brushes are more purpose-specific and are used for oil, acrylic or water-color painting. Specialty brushes for decorative paint finishes can be obtained from local paint dealers or specialty art stores.

All brushes are similarly constructed, although the shape, size and type of bristle may vary. The *filament*, or bristle, is fixed into the *ferrule* (the metal piece holding the filament) with epoxy resin. The handle is attached with rivets or nails. Where the filaments enter the ferrule, *fillers* separate them, allowing the brush to hold more paint. Brushes are made with natural filaments, such as animal hair or bristle, or synthetic filaments, of nylon or polyester. Natural filaments are more durable and give a better paint finish, but are more expensive than brushes with synthetic filaments.

BRUSHES FOR DECORATIVE FINISHES

Standard flat decorators' brushes (1). 2" to 5" (5 to 12.5 cm) wide flat brush for painting walls or large areas.

Sash brushes (2) for painting narrow surfaces and woodwork with oil- or water-based paints. These can also be used for varnishing.

A **cutting brush**, with filaments cut at an angle for edges and corners.

A **specialty oval or flat varnish brush (3)** (which holds a lot of varnish).

A range of **standard round decorators' brushes (4)** for large and small areas.

Artists' fitches (5): flat, round or filbert, natural or synthetic, and used for all fine decorative work in oil or acrylic.

1. Badger softener
Used to soften and blend marks in oil-based and water-based glazes.

2. Japanese hake
Used for softening on small boxes and frames.

5. Flogger
(also used for dragging). Horsehair filaments make it very flexible. Used to flick against wet glaze to create a broken texture resembling wood.

6. Dragger
The filaments are bunched in the ferrule. It may have natural filaments on one side and nylon filaments on the other.

3. Dusting brush
Usually made from hog hair, it can be used for small areas of stippling and softening, but does not work as well as a badger hair brush.

4. Stippling brush
Available in various sizes and used for dispersing glaze evenly over a surface.

CARING FOR BRUSHES
To buy the brushes required for all the finishes described in this book will be costly, so it is important that they are treated well and cleaned thoroughly after having been used.

If your budget allows, try to buy two sets of decorators' brushes – one set for white paint and the other for colors. Some brushes are specifically made for water-based paints and others for oil-based paints. Try to keep these separate because 'water-based' brushes are often made with nylon filaments and will last longer if they are only washed in water.

The first step in brush care is learning to use the brush correctly.

▲▲ When loading the paintbrush with paint (i.e. dipping it into the paint), do not submerge the filaments more than halfway. If paint gets into the filaments where they attach to the ferrule, the brush will be difficult to clean and its lifespan will be shortened.

▲▲ Never stir paint with a brush that you are going to use to paint. Always use a stirring stick, a wooden spoon or a palette knife.

▲▲ You may find that the paint starts clogging and drying at the top of the filaments if you work on a large area. This cannot be helped as, with each brush stroke, the paint will automatically work its way up.

This is when it is advisable to have two brushes. When one brush starts clogging with paint, suspend it in the appropriate solvent to clean it, and continue with the project using the other brush.

▲▲ Most paintbrushes have a hole at the end of the handle; if not, make a hole big enough to take a length of thin wire. When cleaning the brush, suspend the filaments only in the solvent. Do not allow the filaments to rest on the bottom of the container as this will cause them to lose their shape.

▲▲ If you need a break from painting, either suspend the brush in solvent or wrap it in a piece of plastic to prevent it from drying out. Never leave brushes hanging in mineral spirits as the filaments will deteriorate.

Washing brushes

Always wash brushes in the paint's solvent: wash off water-based paint with water, and oil-based paint with mineral spirits.

Wash brushes well at the end of each painting session. Use mild dishwashing liquid and water for the final wash.

Oil-based

▲▲ Prepare two containers of mineral spirits – one for the first wash, to get the bulk of the paint out of the filaments, and the other for the second wash. Squeeze out excess solvent and dry off the brush with a rag before washing it again in the clean solvent.

Suspend brushes after washing.

▲▲ If there is a stubborn residue of paint near the ferrule, take a wire brush and work it through the filaments, away from the ferrule.

▲▲ When all the paint has been washed out in the solvent, wash the brush with mild dishwashing liquid and cold water. Rinse well.

▲▲ Get rid of excess water by rolling the brush's handle between the palms of your hands.

▲▲ Reshape the bristles and hang the brush on a wire hook to dry.

Water-based

▲▲ Using water as the cleaning solvent, rinse the brush under running water, working the paint out of the filaments with your fingers.

▲▲ If there is a stubborn residue of dry paint close to the ferrule, soak the brush in denatured alcohol/

methylated spirits and then use a wire brush to work out the dissolved pieces. Denatured alcohol will only dissolve dried water-based products that have it listed as its solvent, such as shellac.

▲▲ When all the paint has been removed, wash the brush with mild dishwashing liquid and cold water. Rinse well.

▲▲ Get rid of excess water by rolling the brush's handle between the palms of your hands.

▲▲ Reshape the bristles and hang the brush on a wire hook to dry.

Artists' brushes

Never leave artists' brushes standing on their filaments in solvent. This will bend the filaments and make painting with them difficult. Mineral spirits will weaken the filaments if they are left to soak for too long. Always rinse brushes in solvent and let them lie flat between use. Always wash the brushes with soap and water at the end of a working session.

SPECIALTY BRUSHES

If you want specialty brushes to maintain their softness and flexibility, and last a lifetime of painting, treat them as you would your own hair. After the paint has been removed with the appropriate solvent, shampoo and condition the brushes.

Stippling brush

A stippling brush must be dry when you start working with it. Unlike decorators' brushes, a stippling brush cannot be left in solvent during a break or if it starts clogging with paint. The solvent will be absorbed up the length of the filaments and affect the paint finish. Always work with a cloth in hand and wipe the paint off the filaments after a few pounces. If you need to take a break from painting, it is preferable to wash the brush thoroughly and let it dry completely before using it again.

Washing   Work the solvent through the filaments with your fingers and rinse thoroughly. Shampoo and condition. Shake out the excess water and dry the brush with a cloth.

Flogging brush and dragging brush

These brushes can withstand more paint than a stippling brush or badger softener. However, the paint build-up during flogging or dragging must be checked as it will alter the character of the finish. Keep a dry cloth nearby to wipe off excess paint.

Washing   Work the solvent through the filaments with your fingers. Flick out excess solvent and rinse thoroughly. Shampoo and condition.

Softening brushes (badger, hog hair, Japanese hake)

These brushes should never be allowed to gather paint. Only the tips of the filaments should skim the surface of the glaze, softening the glazed surface but without picking up any paint. If excess paint collects on them, it must be washed off so that the quality of the brush is maintained.

Washing   Do not submerge the filaments in solvent for an extended time as it will damage their structure. Work the solvent through the filaments and wipe the brush on a paper towel or cloth. Shampoo and condition, and dry with a hairdryer.

STORING BRUSHES

Some brushes come with a cardboard sleeve and it is advisable to keep them in the sleeve or wrapped in paper once they are dry. This will help to maintain the shape of the filaments.

Specialty brushes

When dry, wrap the brushes in tissue paper or cloth, taking care not to crush the filaments.

Artists' brushes

Take a drop of liquid soap between your thumb and forefinger and coat the filaments with a thin layer. Make sure all the filaments come together to a neat point; the soap will dry and protect them. Stand the brushes, filaments up, in a jar or keep them in a brush pouch.

surface preparation

PREPARING A WORKING SURFACE IS PROBABLY THE MOST IMPORTANT AND TIME-CONSUMING STAGE OF A PROJECT. THE PREPARATION FORMS THE BASE FOR THE LAYERS OF GLAZE AND VARNISH, AND IF THERE IS A DEFECT IN THE BASE, IT WILL CERTAINLY BE VISIBLE IN THE END RESULT. WHETHER YOU ARE WORKING 'ON WALLS OR WOOD, FLOORS OR METAL-WORK – ALL NEED PROPER PREPARATION. THE BASIC RULE OF 'CLEAN, SOUND AND SMOOTH' APPLIES TO ALL SURFACES, BUT THE DEGREE TO WHICH IT IS ACHIEVED DEPENDS ON THE INITIAL STATE OF THE SURFACE.

A collection of surfaces being prepared for repainting or for the application of decorative paint finishes.

SURFACE PREPARATION

THE FIRST STEP IN SURFACE PREPARATION IS TO ESTABLISH EXACTLY WHAT MATERIAL THE SURFACE IS MADE FROM AND THEN TO ASSESS ITS CONDITION. MAKE SURE THAT YOU HAVE ALL THE CORRECT EQUIPMENT READY TO START THE JOB. THIS CHAPTER HAS BEEN DIVIDED INTO DIFFERENT SURFACE CATEGORIES TO MAKE THE SELECTION OF PREPARATION MATERIALS EASY.

WALLS

Pre-painted walls in good condition

If walls are in a good condition minimal preparation is required. However, smoke from tobacco, candles and cooking can leave an invisible oily layer on the surface that will affect the bonding strength of the new base coat. Wash the walls, cornices, rails and baseboards with a solution of TSP (trisodium phosphate) and warm water. Rinse and allow to dry.

Remove unwanted picture hooks and nails, and fill the holes with an all-purpose filler or ready-mixed spackle. When dry, sand the areas and spot-prime with undercoat.

Walls that are in a good condition only need to be washed down with TSP before being painted.

Pre-painted walls in poor condition

If the walls are in poor condition, with peeling paint and large cracks, more preparation work is required. Scrape off the loose paint, ensuring that the plaster is not pulled off. To fill a crack, first enlarge it by inserting the point of a triangular scraper and drawing it along the crack. Dust it out and fill with an all-purpose filler or ready-mixed spackle. If the crack is large, fill it in stages because the compound shrinks as it dries. When dry, sand it smooth and spot-prime the patched area.

Walls pre-painted with an oil-based paint

If the walls have been painted with oil-based paint, rub down the entire wall using a sanding block and sandpaper. This will roughen the surface, creating what is called a *key* or *tooth*, which is essential so that the new layers of paint can bond with the old.

After sanding, the walls should be washed with TSP to remove all traces of dust. The walls are now ready for two coats of either water- or oil-based paint in the base color.

Repair cracks or holes with an all-purpose filler.

To test if a wall has been painted with oil-based or water-based paint, take a rag soaked in denatured alcohol/methylated spirits and rub a spot on the wall in an inconspicuous place. If it is water-based, the paint will dissolve.

New walls

Newly plastered walls do not need to be washed, only lightly dusted. They should be primed with a coat of plaster primer or sealer (ask your paint dealer to recommend an appropriate product as these differ from one manufacturer to another). It is then advisable to apply a coat of universal or all-purpose under-coat. This undercoat is compatible with both oil- and water-based top coats. Even coats of primer and undercoat will make the walls less porous and the top or base coat will be easy to apply. You will also use less paint.

WOODWORK

If you decide to apply a decorative paint finish to a piece of wooden furniture or to wood paneling, the basic rule of having a 'clean, sound and smooth' surface applies.

Wood that is properly prepared guarantees a good, smooth finished product.

Pre-painted woodwork in good condition

Wash this surface with TSP to remove surface dirt. Fill small cracks or nail holes with spackle or wood filler, and sand when dry. Always sand the entire surface regardless of the type of paint used. A good key is always needed on woodwork to allow the new layers of paint to adhere well.

Pre-painted woodwork in poor condition

Try to avoid complete paint removal as it is a very time-consuming and messy operation. Rather, peel off any loose paint with a scraper, trying not to damage the wood, and fill in holes and large cracks with spackle or wood filler. Sand the surface with different grades of sandpaper, ending with the finest grade. If large areas of paint remain, try to sand the edges to make them less visible when top coating. If you choose the paint removal route, use an electric heat stripper as it is less messy and toxic than liquid paint stripper. Once the surface is prepared – either repaired, or completely stripped, washed and sanded – follow the painting procedure for raw wood.

FLOORS

Floors in bad condition do not need as much careful repair as walls, and may be painted to disguise imperfections.

Wooden floors

It is advisable to thoroughly clean wooden floors – either with a sanding machine or using denatured alcohol/methylated spirits and steel wool – to remove old wax polish build-up.

Vacuum the dust, wash the floor with TSP and water, and allow it to dry. Make sure all the nails are hammered in and fill cracks or gaps with wood filler. If you are going to retain the floor's natural color and only work with varnish, choose a wood filler to match the color of the wood or tint it with universal stainer.

The floor will need two coats of water-based primer and one coat of base color. If you are planning a decorative finish or pattern, the base coat should be a low-sheen water- or oil-based paint – whichever is appropriate for the finish.

This wooden floor has been livened up with a painted carpet.

A wooden floor in poor condition.

Raw wood

Give each knot in the wood a few coats of shellac or stain killer paint to seal the wood where natural resins may seep out. This will prevent yellow stains on the painted surface.

Apply a coat of pink or white oil-based wood primer. The oil penetrates the surface, creating a protective layer. When the primer is dry, lightly sand and apply a layer of universal under-coat. Select a base coat paint, color and type depending on the finish you want. Do not paint the base coat using a high-gloss oil paint, unless you are just painting a color with no technique. The best surface to work on is a low-sheen oil- or water-based paint. Apply one or two coats depending on the color. Note that darker colors often require two coats for complete coverage.

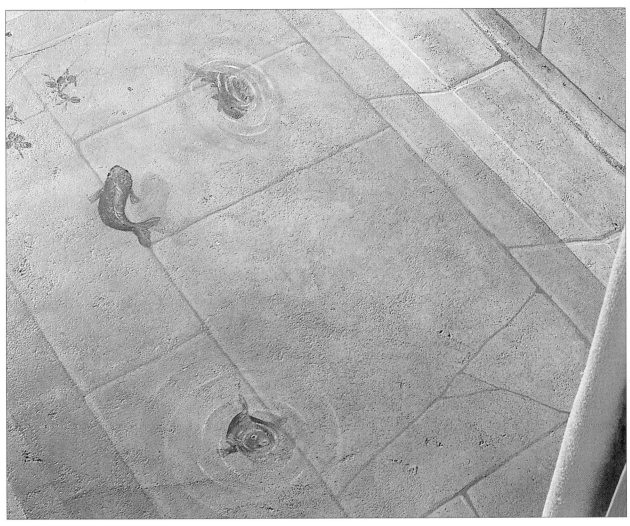

This concrete floor has been creatively painted to represent a fish pond.

When all the paintwork is complete and dry, give the floor at least three or even five thin coats of varnish to ensure durability.

Concrete floors

Concrete floors must be scrubbed with a wire brush and TSP to remove surface grease or loose paint. Remove any sticky glue, left after lifting linoleum or tiles, with a suitable solvent and then wash the area. Trying to fill in small holes or smooth an uneven surface is often problematic and not always successful. If it is very bad, you may have to reskim with new concrete or you may leave it as it is for added character.

It is advisable to use a floor paint manufactured for concrete floors. These are usually oil-based, available in a range of colors and do not have to be finished with a protective varnish. If, however, the color you want is unavailable, and you want a decorative paint finish, have the color specially mixed from appropriate paints. Give the floor one coat of universal undercoat and two coats of the base color. Paint technique the area and then apply four or five coats of polyurethane varnish.

METAL

If you want to paint a metal object, make sure it is free of rust and any loose, peeling paint. Rub it down with fine steel wool or sandpaper. Use a cloth to remove dust. Apply a coat of rust-proofing paint, followed by a coat of metal primer. The item can be painted with any type of paint, but an oil-based paint is recommended.

PLASTIC

Wash the surface to be painted with denatured alcohol/ methylated spirits to remove grease and then wash with strong detergent. Roughen the surface with fine sandpaper and then wipe it with acetone. Apply a layer of universal undercoat or a specific plastic primer (if one is available), then paint on two coats of oil-based paint.

CERAMIC

It is almost impossible to create a tooth or key on a ceramic surface. Prepare the surface by washing it with acetone. Check with your paint supply store whether a ceramic primer or a ceramic-compatible metal primer is available. If not, apply two coats of oil-based paint. As this is not a very stable surface to paint on, peeling can occur with wear and tear. It is not advisable to apply decorative paint finishes to ceramic surfaces, as the finishes are not very durable and will require constant touching up.

DRYING TIMES

Paint drying time varies considerably from one type to another. In general, water-based paint dries faster than oil-based paint. When painting the preparation coats, refer to the instructions and drying time on the paint can. However, it is best to allow 12 to 24 hours between each layer of primer, undercoat and top coat. All paint will reach a surface dryness sooner than indicated. In other words, it will be dry to touch but, below the surface, it will still need time to set and dry before the next layer can be applied.

The drying time of a glaze will determine how much time can be spent working on a decorative finish. Retarders or driers can be added to the glaze to prolong or speed up the drying time, but this will depend on the type of glaze being used and the technique. Always allow a glaze technique to dry thoroughly (12 to 24 hours) before applying the next layer of glaze or varnish.

APPLYING PAINT

When painting an entire room, eliminate unnecessary repairs and tidying up by working in the following order:

- ceiling
- cornices
- walls
- architraves
- windows/window frames
- doors/door frames
- dado rails
- baseboards
- floor (if the floor is being painted).

When painting a floor, remember to work toward a doorway so that you do not become trapped in a corner. Walls should always be painted from the top down; if the paint drips it will fall on an unpainted surface.

Priming

Primers are mostly white. If the base coat is a pale color, leave the primer white as this will give a bright finish. If, however, the base coat is dark, it is advisable to tint the primer with some universal stainer to make it darker. Try to match the hue of the color, but do not attempt to make it as dark. For example, a pale blue or gray primer will be dark enough for a dark blue or mauve base coat. This will also make coverage easier. Remember to use a primer that is compatible with the base coat (i.e. water-based or oil-based). It is always best to apply primer with a brush; it forces the paint into the wall and creates a better sealing and protective layer. However, if the area is too big you can use a short-haired roller and apply a bit more pressure. The primer will dictate the successful application of the base coat layers.

Base coat

This is an important part of any painting process, even if you are not planning a decorative finish. It must be neat, smooth and achieve total coverage.

- The primer coat must be completely dry and the room must be clean and dust-free. Make sure you have all the required equipment: paint trays, rollers, paintbrushes, drop cloth, rags, a mixing bucket and the appropriate solvent. If you are working with water-based paint, have a container of water ready, and if you are using oil-based paint, prepare a container with mineral spirits.

- Paint taken directly from the can is often thick and tends to drip. It is a good idea to dilute the first coat with some of its solvent to achieve an even and smooth finish. Dilute the first coat by about 10 or 15%. Only dilute small quantities at a time to prevent all the paint from drying out. Brush a line of paint neatly along the top cornice, down the corners of the wall, around the door frame and across the dado rail and baseboard. Dip the filaments halfway into the paint and wipe off the excess on the edge. Never overload the brush with paint; rather dip more frequently than have to deal with drips on the walls.

- Pour a small amount of paint into the hollow of the paint tray. Use a long-haired roller made from lambswool, sheepskin or a synthetic equivalent for applying water-based paint. Soak the roller in water and squeeze out the excess. This will

prevent it from absorbing too much paint on the first loading. If using oil-based paint, use a short-haired, smooth-pile roller for a smooth finish.

- Submerge the roller in the paint and roll out the excess on the ridged section behind the paint line. Starting at the top of the wall, roll downward, applying even pressure, but not pressing too hard. Try to cover the wall in a criss-cross pattern. Paint a small section at a time (about 3 sq ft or 1 sq m), first working up and down, and then from side to side. When most of the paint is off the roller, go over the surface again to eliminate any texture or lines. This is called laying off the paint. The process is easier with a brush, but the roller can be controlled in a criss-cross pattern. Don't rush – the result will create a perfect surface for decorative finishes.

PAINT QUANTITIES

It is always a challenge to estimate exactly how much paint is required for a particular job. This will depend on how many coats are required, how absorbent the surface is and the degree to which the paint will be diluted. Here is a rough but fairly accurate guide to buying paint.

When painting a full-strength base coat, 1 quart or liter of paint will cover approximately 100 sq ft or 8 sq m of wall. A wash or glaze will use less paint because it is diluted, therefore 1 quart or liter of glaze will cover approximately 225 sq ft or 20 sq m.

Measure the walls and ceiling in square feet or square meters, and calculate how much paint is required.

color

C OLOR IS ONE OF THE MOST IMPORTANT ASPECTS TO CONSIDER IN

DECORATING A ROOM WITH ANY PAINT FINISH. THIS IS A VERY SUBJECTIVE

CHOICE AND THE FINAL DECISION COULD DEPEND ON SEVERAL FACTORS.

CONSIDER THE FUNCTION OF THE ROOM AND THE ATMOSPHERE YOU WANT

TO CREATE. FOR EXAMPLE, A CHILDREN'S PLAYROOM SHOULD BE BRIGHT,

USING A RANGE OF COLORS THAT INSPIRES CHILDREN TO PLAY AND HAVE

FUN, WHEREAS A STUDY COULD BE MORE SUBDUED, WITH SOFTER, MUTED

COLORS TO CREATE A CALM, QUIET AND RELAXED ATMOSPHERE.

The use of bright and vibrant colors, like those illustrated, can drastically change the atmosphere of a dull room.

BASIC COLOR THEORY

SPECIFIC TERMS ARE USED TO DESCRIBE COLOR. THE WORD *HUE* IS USED TO DISTINGUISH ONE COLOR FROM ANOTHER – FOR EXAMPLE, RED AND GREEN ARE DIFFERENT HUES. THE *PRIMARY COLORS* – RED, BLUE AND YELLOW – ARE ALSO HUES. THESE THREE COLORS ARE CALLED PRIMARY BECAUSE THEY CANNOT BE CREATED BY MIXING OTHER COLORS. HOWEVER, THEY CAN BE MIXED TO CREATE THE *SECONDARY COLORS*: PURPLE, GREEN AND ORANGE. THESE SIX COLORS, PRIMARY AND SECONDARY, ARE THE BASIC COLORS OR HUES OF A STANDARD COLOR WHEEL.

Each primary color lies opposite a secondary color on the color wheel (i.e. red opposite green, yellow opposite purple, and blue opposite orange). These are called *complementary colors*. When these colors are placed next to each other and mixed optically, they stand out and appear brighter. In decorating, a predominantly pink room will often have green introduced in the fabrics or accessories as a complementary color. However, when complementary colors are mixed together as paint, they create a muddy gray color, effectively neutralizing each other.

A *tertiary* color is a mixture of a primary and a secondary color. For example, purple mixed with red will create a reddish purple, or blue mixed with green will create a bluish green.

Color wheel

These colors have altered in hue but are still pure in their depth of color.

By adding white and black to the wheel, a new range of exciting colors emerges. When white is added to a color or hue, it will become paler and is called a *tint*. For example, white added to red will create pink and,

depending on how much white is added, the pink will have a pale or deep *value*. *Tone* is often used in the same context as value and refers to the depth or intensity of color.

When black is added to a color, it becomes darker and is called a *shade*. Again, depending on how much black is added, the color will vary in value.

Colors can be categorized into *warm* and *cool* colors. Warm colors usually refer to reds, oranges and yellows and any colors containing them. However, cool colors can overlap, as seen in the tertiary colors on the color wheel. It is possible to have a warm yellow-green and a cool purple-red.

Earth colors describe a range of colors that are derived from natural pigments found in the earth.

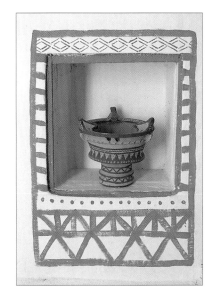

A single color can be as striking as a combination of colors in a room.

Colors like yellow ochre, raw and burnt sienna, raw and burnt umber, Indian red, Venetian red and chrome oxide green are found in clay or stone and, when ground to a powder, can be used with a binder to make paint.

The first artists to make their marks in the form of rock paintings used these pigments and mixed them with animal fat, blood, milk or plant sap to create a usable mixture. Chalk was used for white and carbon for black.

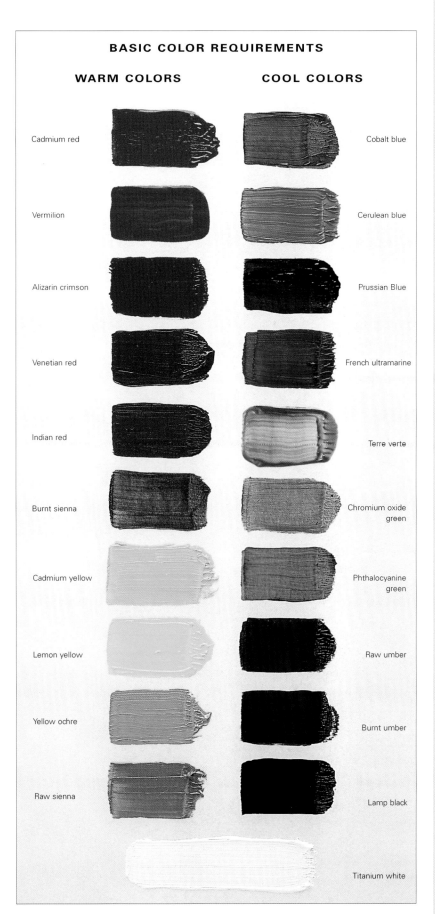

BASIC COLOR REQUIREMENTS

WARM COLORS	COOL COLORS
Cadmium red	Cobalt blue
Vermilion	Cerulean blue
Alizarin crimson	Prussian Blue
Venetian red	French ultramarine
Indian red	Terre verte
Burnt sienna	Chromium oxide green
Cadmium yellow	Phthalocyanine green
Lemon yellow	Raw umber
Yellow ochre	Burnt umber
Raw sienna	Lamp black
	Titanium white

COLOR MIXING

It is important to experiment with mixing paint if you want to create your own colors. Don't be alarmed if you find that mixing paint does not produce the color you thought it would. For example, in theory, two primaries can be mixed to create a secondary color. In practice, the result could be duller than expected. With the development of synthetic pigments, virtually any hue, tint, shade or variation thereof is commercially available. A full range of colors in artists' or students' oils, artists' or students' acrylics, gouache and water-colors can be bought at art stores. The following colors will provide the fullest mixing range:

Reds
Cadmium red
Vermilion
Alizarin crimson
Venetian red
Indian red
Burnt sienna

Yellows
Cadmium yellow
Lemon yellow
Yellow ochre
Raw sienna

Blues
Cobalt blue
Cerulean blue
Prussian blue
French ultramarine

Greens
Terre verte
Chromium oxide green
Phthalocyanine green

Browns
Raw umber
Burnt umber
Van Dyck brown

Titanium white
Payne's gray
Lamp black

Many of these colors are available as universal stainers or tints from hardware and paint supply stores. These can be used to create colors in water-based or oil-based interior and exterior paints.

When mixing colors it is very important to establish which type of paint you are going to use – oil-based paint or water-based paint. Remember to use the appropriate pigments to change colors and the correct solvent to dilute the paint and to clean tools.

Tips on mixing paints

◆ When mixing a pale color or tint, start with a white base and add small quantities of the color. Some colors are stronger than others depending on their pigment composition. If you start with the color and add white to it, you could end up using a lot of white to get it pale enough, and waste paint.

Mixing pale colors.

◆ Black is not always the best color to use to darken a color; it can often change the color completely or make it dull. For example, yellow with added black will turn an olive green. Raw or burnt umber, or even a darker hue in the same family, can be a successful substitute. In the case of yellow, yellow ochre or burnt sienna could be used to create a rich, lively, darker shade.

Black changes yellow to olive green.

◆ If a color is too bright or crisp in its natural state – for example, a bright green – a few drops of its complementary color – in this case, red – can be added and will cause a slight dulling, without making it muddy.

This process will cool a warm color and warm a cool color.

Drops of complementary colors.

◆ Pastel colors pre-mixed by a paint supplier tend to be very 'sweet' and ice-cream-like. A drop of either the complementary color or raw umber will reduce the glare without changing the overall effect of the color.

The following rule applies to water-based and oil-based paints:
◆ Mix pale colors using a brilliant white base.
◆ Mix dark colors using a transparent base or glaze.

Raw umber helps to take the 'sweetness' out of the pastel color.

Using universal stainers to color paint

Universal stainers are the only colorants that can be used in both oil- and water-based paints. They are very easy to use:

1. Add a few drops of the appropriate universal stainer to a container filled with paint (either oil-based or water-based). Remember, if a pale color is required, start with a white base; if a dark color is required, start with a transparent base.

Universal stainer added to water-based scumble glaze.

2. Stir the paint well. Paint a test patch on a piece of card and dry it with a hair dryer. (Oil-based paint will take longer to dry than water-based paint.) At this point you will notice that the dry color is different from the wet color. The degree of difference will depend on the type of paint used and the surface onto which it is applied.

3. Add small quantities of universal stainer until the desired color is achieved.

Using artists' oils to color paint

Artists' oils can only be used to color oil-based paint, glaze and varnish. It is best to use artists' oils when mixing paint for decorative finishes such as tortoiseshell, lapis lazuli and malachite, as they give a much purer color than universal stainers.

1. Squeeze about 1¼ in (3.2 cm) of color or a combination of colors onto a palette. Using a palette knife, mix them together until the desired color is achieved.

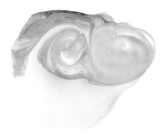

Mixing artists' oils into scumble glaze.

2. Scrape the color mixture into a small bowl or jar and add enough mineral spirits to dilute it to the consistency of thin cream, removing all the lumps.

Diluting artists' oils with mineral spirits to add to glaze.

3. Keep adding a few drops of the color mixture to the base paint (white alkyd or transparent glaze) until the desired color is achieved. A few drops of a drier can be added to the paint to speed up the drying process.

Using artists' acrylic to color paint

Artists' acrylic is a water-based paint that can only be used to color water-based paint, glaze or varnish.

Some acrylic colors are more opaque than others and can produce a cloudy effect when used to stain transparent glaze or varnish.

1. Squeeze about 1¼ in (3.2 cm) of color or a combination of colors onto a palette. Using a palette knife, mix them together until the desired color is achieved.

2. Scrape the color mixture into a small bowl or jar, add enough water to dilute it, and mix it well to remove all the lumps.

Special paint techniques are not always necessary: here bright colors alone have lent these rooms a vibrant, lively atmosphere and have accentuated interior features.

3. Keep adding a few drops of the mixture to the base paint (white paint, transparent glaze or varnish) until the desired color is achieved.

Commercially mixed colors

If you decide not to mix your own colors, you can make use of the vast spectrum of commercially produced colors from a local paint supplier. Most paint manufacturers have devised a system of mixing colors and have coded paint swatches. These are available in a fan deck or as individual swatches. You can use the swatches to match fabrics or existing colors and, when you have reached a decision about the color, a paint supplier will mix up any color needed in the type of paint suitable for the project.

It is advisable to start off with the smallest amount of paint that the store is prepared to mix – usually 1 quart or liter. Paint a sample patch on a sample board or directly onto the wall. A sample board can be made from a smooth piece of hardboard or masonite that has been primed and undercoated with the same products used on the walls. Very often, the color will dry different from the swatch, depending on the type of paint or the wall's surface.

By making a sample board you can check whether the color will work in different lighting – daylight, artificial light at night or in shadow. You can also use the sample board to test decorative techniques. Once you are satisfied with the color and the technique, buy the amount of paint required to complete the project.

A color chart or fan deck shows all the colors that can be mixed commercially.

basic techniques

NOW THAT YOU HAVE COMPLETED ALL THE PREPARATION WORK AND HAVE BOUGHT ALL THE EQUIPMENT REQUIRED, THE FUN CAN BEGIN! LIKE AN ARTIST WITH A NEWLY PRIMED CANVAS, YOU CAN NOW DO ANYTHING YOU WANT TO BY FOLLOWING THE INSTRUCTIONS FOR THE DIFFERENT FINISHES IN THIS CHAPTER. THE MOST IMPORTANT POINTS TO REMEMBER ARE NOT TO BE AFRAID OF MAKING A MISTAKE AND TO ENJOY YOURSELF. THERE IS VERY LITTLE THAT A COAT OF PAINT CANNOT FIX AND, IF NEED BE, YOU CAN ALWAYS START AGAIN.

A range of creative paint finishes, such as the simple color rub technique using different colors and block designs shown here, can transform any room into an exciting space.

COLOR WASHING AND RUBBING

COLOR WASHING AND RUBBING CAN BE DONE ON ROUGH PLASTERED, TEXTURED OR SMOOTH WALLS. A WIDE BRUSH IS USED FOR COLOR WASHING, GIVING A DEFINITE BRUSH STROKE APPEARANCE. COLOR RUBBING IS DONE WITH A CLOTH, WHICH GIVES A SOFTER LOOK. A COLOR WASH ON A ROUGH PLASTERED WALL GENERALLY CREATES THE LOOK OF OLD, FADED TUSCAN OR VENETIAN PLASTER. A COLOR WASH OR COLOR RUB IN SHADES OF RAW SIENNA, YELLOW OCHRE AND BURNT SIENNA IS OFTEN VERY SUCCESSFUL, BUT WHATEVER COLORS ARE USED, THEY MUST BE SIMILAR TONALLY.

MATERIALS

Water-based paint, water, and acrylic scumble glaze
OR
Oil-based paint, mineral spirits, and scumble glaze
Denatured alcohol/methylated spirits
Paintbrushes; 4" (10 cm) bristle, 2" (5 cm) bristle
Wide Japanese hake
Soft, absorbent cloth/sheeting to make cloths
Paint tray
Plastic bag
Latex surgical gloves

PREPARATION

Base coat (water-based paint)
Matte or semi-gloss water-based paint.
A white base coat will give luminosity.

Base coat (oil-based paint)
Oil-based paint.

METHOD

Color washing with a wide brush (water-based paint)

1 Mix together equal quantities of water-based paint and water. If the mixture is too thin, add more paint. Cover the paint tray with a plastic bag and pour some of the paint mixture into the well. (If the plastic bag has printing on it, remember to turn it inside out.) Put on latex surgical gloves.

2 With a bunched cloth or a large brush saturated with water, wet an area of wall approximately 2 sq ft or 60 sq cm.

3 Dab patches of color on the wet wall. Leave a wet border around the section so that it is easy to blend in the next panel.

4 With a dry brush, create a cross-hatched pattern or rainbow-like half-circles that overlap. Every brush stroke should cover the beginning or end of the previous stroke. Wipe the brush with a dry cloth after each stroke.

color washing & rubbing

Distressing and shading color washing

Follow the instructions for color washing with a wide brush. The effect will look as if water has run down the wall. Adding some raw umber universal stainer, which gives a green-brown tint, will simulate moss.

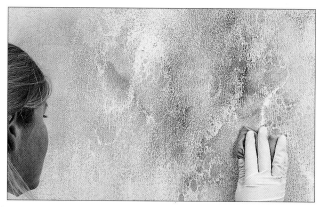

3 Before the paint dries, wipe it with a clean, wet cloth to create a faded effect.

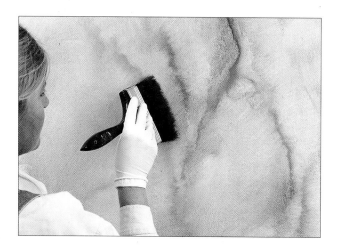

1 After blending the colors, take a dry 2″ (5 cm) or 4″ (10 cm) brush and, while the paint is still wet, start pushing and brushing it to one side. This will build up an irregular and darker pattern. Cross-brush to ensure there is no streaking. Soften with a wide Japanese hake.

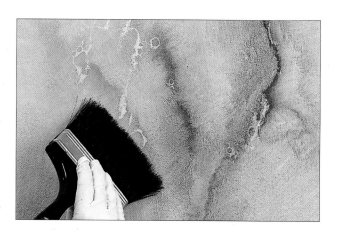

2 Dip your fingers into a container of denatured alcohol/methylated spirits and flick it onto the wet paint. Wait for it to evaporate and then brush over it in all directions using a soft, dry brush to create interesting, crater-like marks.

Remember to leave a wet border around each section so that it is easy to blend in the next panel.

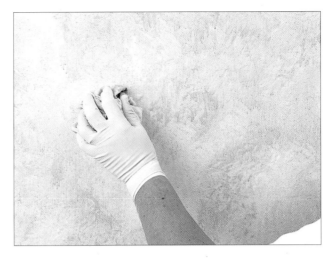

Color rubbing with a cloth (water-based paint)

1 Mix together equal quantities of water-based paint and water. If the mixture is too thin, add more paint. Add acrylic scumble glaze for extended working time. Cover the paint tray with a plastic bag and pour some of the paint mixture into the well. (If the plastic bag has printing on it, remember to turn it inside out.) Put on latex surgical gloves.

2 With a bunched cloth or a large brush saturated with water, wet an area of wall about 2 sq ft or 60 sq cm.

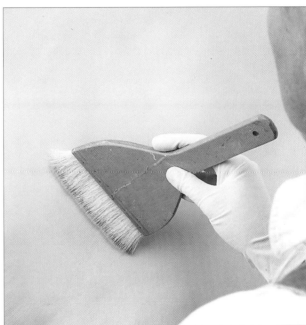

3 Dab patches of color on the wet wall. Leave a wet border around the section so that it is easy to blend in the next panel. Apply the darkest color in a honeycomb pattern, then fill in the gaps with one or two lighter colors.

4 Blend the colors with a damp cloth pad using a twisting action. Start with the palest color and then the darker color until they are blended. Continued rubbing results in a softer effect, or soften with a hake brush.

Allow 24 hours for the first coat to dry before doing a second or third rubbing.

Color rubbing with a cloth (oil-based paint)

1 Follow the instructions (above) for color rubbing but use oil-based glaze. Work on a dry wall.

These walls have been color rubbed with a neutral stone shade to enhance this room's gracious and traditional ambience.

Color washing with a wide brush (oil-based paint)

1 Mix together equal quantities of oil-based paint and mineral spirits. Alternatively, for extended working time, mix together equal quantities of oil-based paint, mineral spirits and scumble glaze. Cover the paint tray with a plastic bag and pour some of the paint mixture into the well. (If the plastic bag has printing on it, remember to turn it inside out.) Put on latex surgical gloves.

2 Dab patches of color on the wall and blend with a dry wide brush.

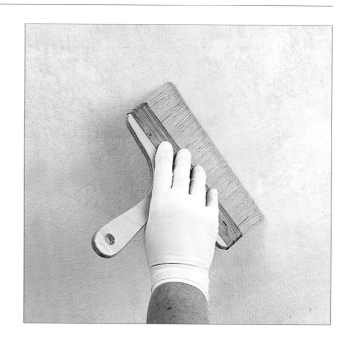

An earthy colored wash on these walls contrasts well with the stark white furniture.

DRAGGING

Dragging is the most challenging, but also one of the most beautiful, paint techniques. When it is well done, it looks like silk. Fine vertical lines result from the brush being dragged through the glaze. It is very effective on doors and on furniture. To paint a room requires two people — one laying on the paint and the other dragging.

MATERIALS

Equal quantities of oil-based paint, mineral spirits, and scumble glaze

Paintbrush; 2" (5 cm)

Short-haired paint roller

Dragging brush

Cloths; about 2 sq ft or 60 sq cm

Plumb line

Paint tray

Plastic bag

This method could also be used with water-based emulsion paint, acrylic scumble glaze and water in equal quantities.

PREPARATION

Base coat

Walls painted with oil-based paint must be washed with a solution of TSP and water to remove traces of grease. Rinse the walls with clean water. When dry, sand with medium-grade sandpaper.

Newly painted walls must be sanded with medium-grade sandpaper. The walls must be very smooth, otherwise the glaze collects in indentations and the dragged lines may go askew.

METHOD

1 Mix together equal quantities of oil-based paint, mineral spirits and scumble glaze. Cover the paint tray with a plastic bag and pour some of the paint mixture into the well. (If the plastic bag has printing on it, remember to turn it inside out.)

3 Dip the roller into the glaze and roll out the excess on the flat part of the paint tray. Start rolling the glaze on the wall in a 12" (30.5 cm) wide vertical panel.

2 Dip a 2" (5 cm) paintbrush into the glaze and, starting in a corner, paint a vertical strip down the wall from below the cornice to above the baseboard.

4 'Butter' the dragging brush by putting a little glaze onto it with the 2" (5 cm) paintbrush.

WARNING

Cloths saturated with glaze must not be put into a plastic bag and closed. This can result in spontaneous combustion, as the combination of paint, mineral spirits and scumble glaze has a low flash point. Spread the cloths out to dry completely before throwing them away.

5 Position the dragging brush on the wall in the corner, against the ceiling or cornice. Push it firmly against the wall and drag it down using even pressure. If the wall is high, use a ladder and step down while dragging.

7 After each drag, wipe the brush with a clean, dry cloth to remove the glaze lifted off the wall.

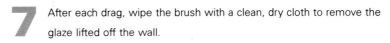

6 Lift the brush away from the wall at the baseboard. Place the brush with bristles down above the baseboard and pull it up to join the downward drag. Lift brush off the wall.

8 The second person lays on the next panel of glaze, two rollers wide. Drop a plumb line from the top of the wall to ensure the dragged panels are vertical. Continue laying on and dragging until the wall is complete.

dragging

A brush-drag technique has been applied to this wall from cornice to dado line. The color selection was based on the fabric.

CLOTH DRAGGING

CLOTH DRAGGING CREATES A COARSER, MORE DEFINITE STRIPE. IT IS VERY EFFECTIVE AND QUITE DRAMATIC WHEN TWO COLORS ARE USED. THERE WILL ALWAYS BE AN UNTIDY EDGE AT THE START AND FINISH. THIS CAN BE COVERED WITH A PAINTED BORDER STRIP.

MATERIALS

Equal quantities of water-based
    paint, acrylic scumble glaze,
    and water
Cloths; about 2 sq ft or 60 sq cm
Plumb line
Paint tray
Plastic bag
Latex surgical gloves
Bucket of water (to rinse cloths)

PREPARATION

Base coat

Matte or semi-gloss water-based paint. Semi-gloss is preferable, as the top coat will not dry as quickly. Walls painted with water-based paint or oil-based paint must be washed down with a solution of TSP and water to remove traces of grease. Rinse the walls with clean water. This is particularly important as any grease residue will break up the dragging stripes and result in unpainted patches.

METHOD

1 Mix together equal quantities of paint, scumble glaze and water.

Cover the paint tray with a plastic bag and pour some of the paint mixture into the well. (If the plastic bag has printing on it, remember to turn it inside out.) Put on the latex surgical gloves.

2 Soak a cloth in the bucket of water and wring it out well.

3 Dip the cloth into the paint and squeeze out the excess on the flat part of the paint tray. Bunch the cloth in your hand, pushing it between your fingers, and start dragging from the top of the wall toward the baseboard.

4 When you reach the dado rail or baseboard, lift the cloth away from the wall. Drag up to join the downward stroke. Drop a plumb line from the top of the wall to ensure the dragged panels are vertical.

5 Drag the next panel with the same or a second color.

Equal quantities of oil-based paint, mineral spirits and scumble glaze can be used instead.

BRUSH DRAGGING

THE FINELY LINED FINISH OF BRUSH DRAGGING WORKS BEST ON FLAT SURFACES; UNEVEN SURFACES DISTORT THE BRUSH AND RUIN THE EFFECT.

MATERIALS

Water-based paint, water, and
   acrylic scumble glaze
Water-based or polyurethane varnish
Dragging brush; 4" to 12"
   (10 to 30.5 cm)
Paintbrush; 2" (5 cm) or short-
   haired mohair roller (depending
   on size of project)
Cloths
Masking tape
Paint tray covered with plastic bag

PREPARATION

Base coat
Semi-gloss water-based emulsion paint. Do not use matte paint because it is too absorbent for this technique.

METHOD

1 Mix together equal quantities of paint, water and acrylic scumble glaze. Pour some of the paint mixture into the paint tray.

2 Look at the corner construction (in this example it is at right angles). Using masking tape, mask off the vertical sides on the join of the wood. Dip a 2" (5 cm) paintbrush or roller into the paint and paint the two vertical sides. Allow the paint to set up slightly and drag where you have painted from top to bottom.

3 Gently remove the masking tape and clean any paint that might have bled under the tape. When dry, repeat the process, masking off the horizontal strips.

4 The center has been treated with a ragging technique and the edges of the molding stippled and wiped clean with a cloth.

5 Cupboard doors must be varnished with two coats of water-based or polyurethane varnish.

6 If the panels or doors have been constructed with a 45° or mitered join, place the masking tape at a 45° angle to the join and follow the painting instructions.

This method could also be used on cupboard doors in kitchens and bathrooms using oil-based paint, mineral spirits and scumble glaze in equal quantities.

A beautiful brush-dragged finish on kitchen cupboards.

FLOGGING

FLOGGING IS A SIMPLE TECHNIQUE THAT INVOLVES PUSHING, DRAGGING OR PATTING A FLOGGING BRUSH INTO A GLAZE TO CREATE A WOODGRAIN EFFECT. IT IS AN INTERESTING FINISH IN ANY COLOR AND WORKS WELL ON FLAT SURFACES. THE WOODGRAIN APPEARANCE LOOKS EFFECTIVE ON PANELED WALLS AND CUPBOARD DOORS.

MATERIALS

Equal quantities of oil-based paint, mineral spirits, and scumble glaze

Brush; 2″ (5 cm) or smooth-haired roller

Long-haired bristle flogging brush

Soft cloth wrapped around a spackle blade

PREPARATION

Base coat
Oil-based paint.

METHOD

1 Mix together equal quantities of oil-based paint, mineral spirits and scumble glaze.

2 Apply the glaze mixture using a brush or a roller.

4 When a single brush-width panel has been painted, turn the flogger facedown and, with short strokes, fill in the gap below the starting point.

3 Holding the flogging brush firmly, start flogging upward (working from bottom to top). Slap the flogger against the wall in short overlapping movements.

5 Clean the baseboard with a soft cloth wrapped around a spackle blade. Lay on the next panel of glaze and continue flogging.

A fantasy wood-grained panel surrounds this sumptuous room.

FLOGGING WITH WATER-BASED POWDER PIGMENT AND VINEGAR

THE ADVANTAGES OF FLOGGING WITH WATER-BASED POWDER PIGMENTS ARE THAT THEY DRY IMMEDIATELY AND ALLOW OIL-BASED GLAZE TO BE PAINTED OVER FOR WOODGRAINING. THEY CAN THEN BE SEALED WITH POLYURETHANE VARNISH.

MATERIALS

Powder pigment (color of choice)

Van Dyck brown powder pigment
   (optional, for mahogany)

Whiting powder

Cider vinegar or malt vinegar

Artists' oil color, mineral spirits,
   and scumble glaze (optional)

Polyurethane varnish or shellac

Flogging brush

Brush; ¾" to 2" (2 to 5 cm),
   depending on size of project

Medium-grade sandpaper

Cloth

PREPARATION

Base coat
Oil-based paint.

METHOD

1 Sand the object or furniture to be painted with sandpaper. Mix enough whiting powder with a little water to form a runny paste.

2 Dip a cloth into the whiting mixture and rub over the surface using a circular movement. This allows the oil-based coat to accept the water-based medium without beading.

3 Mix one part powder pigment with two parts vinegar in a small dish. If it is too dark add more vinegar. (For mahogany, use Van Dyck brown powder pigment. It is very strong, so use it sparingly.) Stir the mixture to prevent the powder settling (it does not dissolve completely).

4 Paint the mixture onto the object, furniture or panel and begin flogging. As it dries very quickly, keep flogging if you want a fine finish. Do not overdo flogging as this could eliminate all the marks. If the finish is unsuccessful, wipe it off with a wet cloth and start again.

5 To preserve this fragile finish, seal it either with polyurethane varnish or with shellac.

6 If this finish is a first working for wood graining, work over it with an oil-based glaze of artists' oil color, mineral spirits and scumble glaze before sealing it with polyurethane varnish.

flogging

RAGGING

RAGGING ON HAS A SOFT, CRUSHED-VELVET APPEARANCE DEPENDING ON THE CLOTH OR 'RAG' USED TO APPLY THE PAINT MIXTURE. RAG ROLLING HAS A CRISPER APPEARANCE, SIMILAR TO FORMICA, BUT CAN BE SOFTENED BY APPLYING SEVERAL LAYERS IN LIGHTER SHADES. RAGGING ON CAN BE DONE VERY OPENLY — LEAVING MUCH OF THE BASE COLOR SHOWING — OR QUITE DENSELY, CREATING A MORE SOLID APPEARANCE.

MATERIALS

Water-based paint, water, and
   acrylic scumble glaze
OR
Oil-based paint, scumble glaze, and
   mineral spirits
Small can of base color
Small paintbrush or fitch
Rags: soft sheeting or fine cotton-
   knit (T-shirt) fabric, each rag to
   measure about 2 sq ft or 60 sq cm
Pieces of brown paper
Pieces of cardboard
Latex surgical gloves

PREPARATION

Base coat

Oil-based paint or water-based paint.
Newly painted walls can either be a
matte or semi-gloss.

METHOD

Ragging on

1 *Water-based paint:* Mix together equal quantities of paint, water and acrylic scumble glaze, to achieve a consistency like that of thin cream.
Oil-based paint: Mix together equal quantities of oil-based paint, mineral spirits and scumble glaze to form a smooth glaze.
Put on the latex surgical gloves.

2 *Water-based paint:* Soak a rag in water and wring it out. Damp cloth absorbs the paint mixture more easily. Dip the damp rag into the paint mixture and wring out excess paint. Ensure there is no dripping.
Oil-based paint: Saturate the rag with glaze and squeeze out excess paint. Ensure there is no dripping.

3 Gather the edges of the rag and bunch the cloth into a 'rose'. Push indentations into the cloth with your fingers to give it a crushed appearance. Test the pattern and the amount of paint mixture or glaze on the rag by pouncing it on a piece of brown paper. Try to get a uniform pattern rather than a solid block of color.

4 Start ragging at the top of the wall, getting as close as possible to the corners and cornice. Rag on with a definite but light pouncing movement. Pounce randomly, rather than in rows, as the rag has a distinctive pattern. It helps to move your whole arm, not only your wrist, to cover a wider area of wall. Check that the cloth retains its indentations to create the pattern and is not flattened by the pouncing. Do not twist the cloth on the wall as this will smudge the pattern. Work in an area of about 2 sq ft or 60 sq cm.

5 With edges like a jigsaw puzzle, work down the wall in a checkerboard pattern, then go back up to the top and fill in the blank spaces.

6 *Water-based paint:* Rinse the cloth in water when it becomes slimy with paint, then wring it out and start again. Alternatively, use a new rag.
Oil-based paint: When the rag is saturated, it must be replaced. Have a good supply of rags available.

7 To finish the room, fill in the corners and the sections above the baseboard and below the cornice. Hold a piece of cardboard against the cornice and fill in the gaps by dabbing gently with a small piece of paint- or glaze-filled cloth bunched between your fingers. Do the same in the corners and above the baseboard.

8 Stand back and look at the wall to make sure that a uniform effect has been achieved. Where there are gaps, fill them with a small rag or brush dipped in the paint or glaze mixture. If the ragging smudged or was applied too heavily in some areas, use the undiluted base coat to touch up and rectify mistakes.

Allow the first color to dry thoroughly before applying a second or third working. Remember, the last coat will be the dominant color.

ragging

Rag rolling

1 Follow steps 1 and 2 for ragging on (*see* page 52).

2 Bunch and roll the cloth into a thick sausage. Holding it in your fingertips, test the pattern and the amount of paint or glaze mixture on the rag by rolling it on a piece of brown paper.

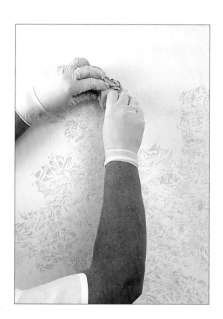

3 Place the rag on the wall and, working upward, roll it away from you in different directions. Do not pull the cloth toward you as the effect will smudge. Work in an area of about 2 sq ft or 60 sq cm. With edges like a jigsaw puzzle, work down the wall in a checkerboard pattern, then go back up to the top and fill in the blank spaces. Work into the corner with a smaller, bunched cloth.

4 ***Water-based paint:*** Rinse the cloth in water when it becomes slimy with paint, wring it out and start again. Alternatively, use a new cloth.
Oil-based paint: Discard the saturated cloth and start with a new piece.

5 Follow steps 7 and 8 for ragging on (*see* page 53).

WARNING

Rags saturated with glaze must not be put into a plastic bag and closed. This can result in spontaneous combustion, because scumble glaze mixed with mineral spirits has a low flash point. Spread the rags out to dry completely before throwing them away.

Ragging in soft colors creates a subtle mottled effect.

SOLVENT RELEASE

SOLVENT RELEASE SIMPLY MEANS THAT THE SOLVENT REACTS WITH AND DISSOLVES THE LAYER OF PAINTED GLAZE APPLIED OVER THE BASE COLOR, CREATING A CRATERED EFFECT.

MATERIALS

Oil-based paint, mineral spirits, and
    scumble glaze
OR
Water-based paint and water
Solvent
Short-haired bristle brush; No. 9 or 11
Badger brush or Japanese hake
Paintbrush; 2 in (5 cm)

SOLVENTS AND THEIR USES IN DECORATIVE PAINTING

Mineral spirits

Distilled from crude petroleum oils. Used on a paint and scumble glaze mixture over an oil-based base coat.

Benzine or Naphtha

A petroleum distilled solvent used on a paint and scumble glaze mixture over an oil-based base coat.

Denatured alcohol/methylated spirits

Used on diluted water-based paints over a semi-gloss water-based base coat.

METHOD

Solvent release craters (oil-based paint)

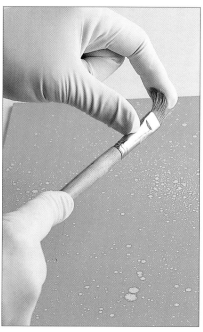

1 Mix together equal quantities of oil-based paint, mineral spirits and scumble glaze, and paint over an oil-based base coat. Pour a small amount of the solvent into a dish.

2 Dip the bristle brush into the mineral spirits and spatter the wet glaze. The solvent will 'eat away' at the glaze, forming small craters.

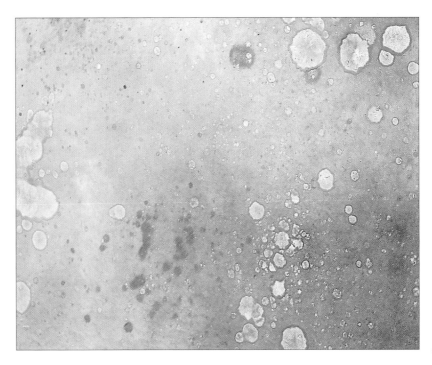

3 For a cloudy effect, soften the craters with a badger brush or Japanese hake. Softening polishes the surface and blends hard edges.

Fossil stone or stone finishes

Spattering with mineral spirits can be very effective in creating holes in stone finishes. Benzine or naphtha is used when bigger holes or craters are required. It can be dabbed or flicked on with a small brush.

Solvent release craters (water-based paint)

1 Mix equal quantities water-based paint and water. Paint it over a semi-gloss water-based base coat.

Because the paint dries quickly, denatured alcohol/methylated spirit is used as a solvent to create the craters.

2 Dip the bristle brush into the denatured alcohol/ methylated spirits and spatter the painted surface.

3 Soften with a Japanese hake to reveal the craters. Allow time for the solvent to react with the paint and then brush it with a 2″ (5 cm) brush before it dries. This will result in dark ringed holes that look like old marks.

Different sizes of holes or craters can be achieved using a variety of solvents.

SPATTERING

OBJECTS AND FURNITURE CAN BE SPATTERED SUCCESSFULLY, EITHER ENTIRELY OR PARTIALLY, TO CREATE A 'SPECKLED' APPEARANCE THAT WILL GIVE A FAUX ANTIQUE OR AGED FINISH MORE AUTHENTICITY. TO SAVE TIME, COMMERCIAL SPRAY EQUIPMENT SHOULD BE USED TO SPATTER LARGE AREAS SUCH AS WALLS.

MATERIALS

Water-based paint, oil-based paint, or artists' oil color diluted with mineral spirits can be used for spattering.

Paint and solvent mixed on a small plate to form a thin cream
Bristle brush; No. 12
Comb
Brush or stick
Latex surgical gloves

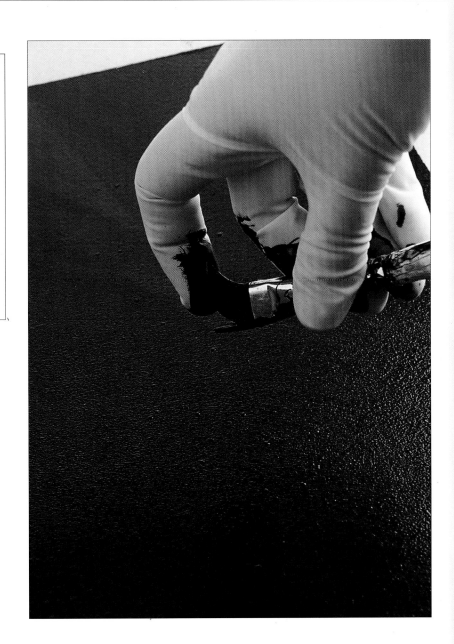

PREPARATION

Base coat
Water-based paint or oil-based paint.

METHOD

Finger spattering

1 Dip the paintbrush into the paint and dab out any excess on the plate.

2 Hold the brush upright between thumb and fingers, and use your index finger to spatter the paint by pulling back and then releasing the bristles.

Finger spattering with a comb

1 Dip the comb into the paint and dab out any excess on the plate. Pull your finger over the teeth of the comb.

Tapping

1 Dip the paintbrush into the paint and dab out any excess on the plate.

2 Stand over the object and tap the loaded paintbrush against a stick or another paintbrush.

Spattering with a few colors creates a faux granite finish.

Simple, one-color spattering enhances this lamp base.

Spattering has been used extensively on these frames to make them appear aged.

SPONGING

Sponging is a very quick and effective way of changing the color of a room by applying one or more colors over the base coat. Colors that are tonally similar to the background, rather than contrasting, will produce the best results. Depending on which side of the sponge is used, the effect can be either finely or coarsely mottled. Sponging layer upon layer produces a cloudy effect.

MATERIALS

Water-based paint and water

OR

Oil-based paint and mineral spirits

Small can of base color

Bucket of solvent

Large natural sea sponge*

Small natural sea sponge*

(Commercially manufactured synthetic sponges can be used with pieces picked out of them to create an irregular pattern. Use sponges with various sized holes rather than flat foam sponges.)

Small paintbrush or fitch

Pieces of brown paper

Pieces of cardboard

Paint tray

Plastic bag

Latex surgical gloves

Soap and water

PREPARATION

Base coat (water-based paint)

Newly painted or previously painted walls with either a matte or a semi-gloss finish.

Base coat (oil-based paint)

Newly painted or previously painted walls with either an eggshell or a semi-gloss finish. When dry, sand lightly with fine-grade sandpaper to remove the sheen and to ensure the sponging adheres to the surface.

METHOD

1 Mix together equal quantities of paint and solvent. Test the mixture on the wall; if it runs it is too thin and more paint must be added to make it thicker. Cover the paint tray with a plastic bag and pour some of the paint mixture into the well. (If the plastic bag has printing on it, turn it inside out.) Put on the latex surgical gloves.

2 Soak the large sponge in the bucket of solvent. Squeeze out all the solvent so that the sponge is only damp. Never dip a dry sponge directly into paint.

3 Dip the sponge into the paint mixture and squeeze out the excess on the flat part of the paint tray.

4 Cupping the sponge in your hand, test the pattern and the amount of paint mixture in it by pouncing it on a piece of brown paper. The pattern will either appear as a fine stippled effect or, by using the 'brain' side of the sponge, a definite coarse and open pattern. Always use the same area of sponge.

6 ***Water-based paint:*** Wash the sponge frequently in water to prevent it from clogging with paint. Squeeze it out, then start again.

Oil-based paint: Wash the sponge frequently in mineral spirits to prevent it from clogging with paint. Squeeze out excess mineral spirits, then wash the sponge with soap and water and start again. If the sponge is not washed in soap and water, the mineral spirits will dilute the paint mixture.

5 Start sponging the wall from the top, getting as close as possible to the corners and cornice. Sponge with a definite but light pouncing movement. Do not pounce in rows as each sponge has a distinctive pattern and the effect will be similar to a potato print. It helps to move your whole arm, not only your wrist, to cover a wider area of wall. Work on an area of about 2 sq ft or 60 sq cm. With edges like a jig-saw puzzle, work down the wall in a checkerboard pattern, then go back up to the top and fill in the blank spaces.

7 To finish the room, fill in the corners and the sections above the baseboard and below the cornice. Hold a piece of cardboard against the cornice and sponge up to it using the small sponge. Do the same in the corners and above the baseboard.

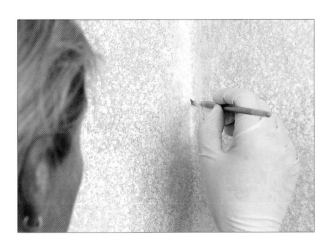

8 Stand back and look at the wall to make sure that a uniform surface effect has been achieved. Where there are gaps, fill them using a small brush dipped in the paint mixture.

9 If the sponging smudged or was applied too heavily in some areas, use the undiluted base coat paint and a sponge or brush to touch up and rectify mistakes.

10 If you are using more than one color, repeat the procedure. Remember, the last coat will be the dominant color.

Two colors have been used effectively in this bathroom.

A very pale color sponged onto this wall gives a perfect background for a mural like this angel painted in one color.

Using a dark color has given this attic bathroom a rich, warm atmosphere.

Sponging only specific areas, such as the stenciled key-pattern border around this bathroom's walls, can be highly effective.

STIPPLING

STIPPLING IS A PAINT FINISH RESEMBLING FINE DOTS. IT ELIMINATES BRUSH STROKES AND CREATES A UNIFORM EFFECT. IT IS SUITABLE FOR WALLS, FURNITURE, ORNAMENTS, AND PARTICULARLY FOR MOLDINGS AND CURVED SURFACES.

MATERIALS

Oil-based paint or artists' oil paint

Mineral spirits

Scumble glaze

Specialty brushes (size needed depends on the project):

Bristle brush	No. 8 round bristle
	No. 9 round bristle
Edge stipplers	4" x 1" (10 x 2.5 cm)
	6" x 1" (15 x 2.5 cm)
Block stipplers	6" x 2" (15 x 5 cm)
	4" x 3" (10 x 7.5 cm)
	6" x 5" (15 x 12.5 cm)
Dusting brush	4" x 1" (10 x 2.5 cm)
Flat nylon brush	1¼" (3.2 cm)
Softener	
Decorators' brushes	2" (5 cm)
	4" (10 cm)

Short-haired roller

Paint tray

Plastic bag

Soft cloths

Cotton swab

PREPARATION

Base coat

Oil-based paint.

- Only walls in a very good condition should be stippled, as the glaze will collect in and accentuate any imperfections.
- This technique requires two people – one to lay on and one to stipple. It is important to keep painting until the room is complete.

METHOD

Walls

1 Mix together equal quantities of oil-based paint, mineral spirits and scumble glaze. Alternatively, mix together artists' oil color diluted with mineral spirits and add an equal amount of scumble glaze to form the consistency of thick cream. Cover the paint tray with a plastic bag and pour some of the glaze into the well. (If the plastic bag has printing on it, turn it inside out.)

Right: Stippling created a subtle background for this simple trompe l'oeil *molding.*

2 Dip a 2″ (5 cm) bristle brush into the glaze and, starting in a corner, paint a vertical strip down the wall from below the cornice to above the baseboard.

4 'Butter' the block stippler so that the first pounce does not remove too much glaze. The brush must be held with the bristles at right angles to the wall.

6 Stipple in corners using a small edge stippler.

3 Dip the roller into the glaze and roll out the excess on the flat part of the paint tray. Start rolling the glaze on the wall in a 2 ft or 60 cm wide vertical panel.

5 Stipple the wall with a punching action, moving your hand in a circular pattern to overlap the imprint. Work downward from the cornice to the baseboard.

7 While the first person stipples, the second person lays on the next panel of glaze. It is important to leave an unstippled wet edge where a new panel will be joined. Paint the new panel up to the wet edge. Do not overlap the panels too much as this will create a visible line.

8 After painting each panel, wipe the block stippler with a clean dry cloth to remove excess glaze. Use a cloth dipped in mineral spirits to remove glaze on the baseboard or cornice.

Ornaments (pots, wooden objects, frames, lamps, etc.)

1 If the object is molded or circular, it is advisable to paint the glaze on thinly and evenly using a 1¼″ (3.2 cm) flat nylon brush. Stipple evenly around the object using a small softener or a stippling brush. Even a 2″ (5 cm) decorators' brush can be used if the bristles are cut short.

2 Wipe the raised areas with a clean cloth.

Moldings and carved furniture

1 Apply the glaze to moldings or carved areas using a 2″ (5 cm) decorators' brush or a 1¼″ (3.2 cm) flat nylon brush, depending on the size of the object.

2 Finely stipple the molding with a small stippling brush. The more you stipple, the lighter the stippling will become.

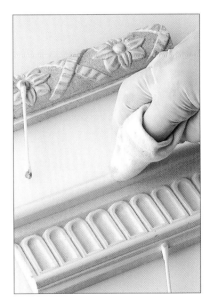

3 Make a pad from a clean piece of soft cloth and gently wipe along the molding using short strokes. A cotton swab can be used for finer sections, depending on how much glaze needs to be removed. If a harsh line results from wiping the molding, it can be softened with the stippling brush.

ANTIQUING WITH STIPPLING

STIPPLING CAN BE USED TO CREATE A DELICATE AND ELEGANT ANTIQUED EFFECT BY APPLYING A COAT OF ANTIQUING GLAZE OVER A NEWLY PAINTED OR BRIGHT GOLD OBJECT AND THEN STIPPLING TO ELIMINATE BRUSH STROKES.

MATERIALS

Raw umber or burnt umber artists'
   oil color
Mineral spirits
Scumble glaze
Drier (to accelerate the drying rate)
Bristle brush; No. 12
Large block stippler
Edge stippler
Squirrel hair brush; No. 8
Soft cloths
Rottenstone or clay dust

PREPARATION

Base coat
Alkyd eggshell enamel

METHOD

1 Squeeze about 2" (5 cm) of raw umber or burnt umber artists' oil
color into a small container. Add an equal amount of mineral spirits, mix well,
and then add an equal amount of scumble glaze. The mixture should be the
consistency of thin cream.

2 Add 1–2 drops of drier to the required amount of antiquing glaze
(not to the entire mixture). Paint the glaze onto the object.

3 Allow the glaze to 'set up' or dry a little, then stipple using the big block stippler. This eliminates brush strokes.

5 Stipple the wiped edges with a smaller stippler to soften them.

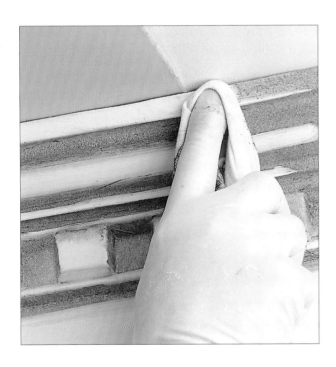

4 Wipe the raised sections of the carving or molding with a soft cloth or pad. If you want to remove more of the glaze, dip the cloth in a little mineral spirits.

6 For an old and dusty look, dust some rottenstone or clay dust into the indentations while the antiquing glaze mixture is still wet, using a soft No. 8 squirrel hair brush.

decor finishes

DECOR FINISHES REQUIRE MORE ADVANCED SKILLS, BUT MOST OF

THEM MAKE USE OF THE BASIC TECHNIQUES TO CREATE FAUX STONE

FINISHES AND EXOTIC SURFACES. MANY OF THESE FINISHES ARE

RESERVED FOR SMALLER OBJECTS, TRINKET BOXES, FRAMES, LAMP

BASES, OR PANELING ON WALLS AND DOORS. THEY ARE OFTEN USED IN

RESTORATION PROJECTS. FOR EXAMPLE, IF A MARBLE BASEBOARD HAS

BEEN PARTIALLY DESTROYED AND THE OLD MARBLE CAN NO LONGER BE

MINED, ARTISTS CAN SIMULATE IT USING PAINT.

*A combination of decorative
finishes and faux marbling
can be used to camouflage
or enhance interior structures
and furnishings.*

FAUX LACQUER

FAUX LACQUER IS A HIGHLY POLISHED GLOWING GLAZE IN TWO OR MORE SHADES OR SIMILAR COLORS. IT IS USED VERY SUCCESSFULLY TO SIMULATE LEATHER IN TONES OF BROWN.

MATERIALS

Artists' oil paint in two or more shades/colors – for example, alizarin crimson and burnt umber, or monestial green and burnt umber, or, for leather, burnt sienna and burnt umber

Mineral spirits

Scumble glaze

Gold or bronze powder

Polyurethane gloss varnish

Drier

Decorators' brushes (one for each color)

Wall:	4" or 5" (10 or 12.5 cm)
Table top:	2" (5 cm)
Small object:	1" (2.5 cm)

Stippling brush

Badger brush or Japanese hake

Soft squirrel hair brush

Flat varnish brush

Very fine cotton-knit fabric, fiberfill, and rubber band

Fine-grade sandpaper

PREPARATION

Base coat

Faux lacquer requires a very smooth surface, painted with an oil-based base coat. It is best to use either white or a pastel shade of the color you intend using.

METHOD

1 Mix together the first artists' oil color and a small quantity of mineral spirits to the consistency of thick cream, adding more only when the lumps have dissolved. Add an equal amount of scumble glaze to the mixture to achieve a consistency of thin cream. The amount of artists' oil color used depends on the strength of color required. A tube of artists' oil color will require about one cup of mineral spirits and one cup of scumble glaze. Mix the second color in the same way.

2 Add a few drops of a drier to a portion of the glaze (not the entire mixture because the glaze will set before it can be used). Three drops of drier to a half-cup of glaze should be enough.

3 With the small decorators' brush dab patches of the lighter colored glaze onto the surface of the box.

4 Fill in with smaller patches of the darker colored glaze. When both colors have been applied they can be blended with a cotton bob or a stipple brush so that there are no patches. A 'bob' is made from cotton-knit fabric wrapped around fiberfill and secured with a rubber band (see page 81).

5 Use a stipple brush to stipple the lighter color and eliminate brush strokes, then blend it into the darker color.

7 For decorative effect, gold or bronze powder can be scattered onto the wet glaze. Dip a soft squirrel hair brush into the powder and tap it lightly over the glaze. Allow the glaze to dry, then blow away any excess powder.

6 Soften or polish the surface with a badger brush or Japanese hake, brushing in all directions.

WARNING

Gold and bronze powders are made from ground metal and are dangerous if inhaled. Wear a paper mask over your mouth and nose when working with these materials.

8 When the faux lacquer effect is completely dry, varnish with two coats of polyurethane gloss. The first coat of varnish can be thinned with 20% mineral spirits. When dry, smooth bumps or dust particles with very fine sandpaper and apply a second coat of varnish.

If you are using this technique on walls or large surfaces, work in an area measuring roughly 2 sq ft or 60 sq cm. Paint the next panel into the wet edge of the completed area and repeat the process.

The ceiling of this spacious entrance hall has been painted in a faux lacquer finish, optically reducing the height of the walls.

LAPIS LAZULI

Lapis lazuli is a bright, azure blue gemstone, often flecked with gold specks of iron pyrites. It was once used as a paint pigment for ultramarine blue.

MATERIALS

Ultramarine blue artists' oil color

Prussian blue artists' oil color

Mineral spirits

Scumble glaze

Gold powder

Gloss polyurethane varnish

Drier

Stippling brush

Badger brush or Japanese hake

Flat bristle brush

Flat varnish brush

2 small natural sea sponges

Cotton-knit fabric, fiberfill and
    rubber band

Fine-grade sandpaper

PREPARATION

Base coat

Pale ultramarine blue, oil-based paint.
The surface must be very smooth.

METHOD

1 Mix the ultramarine blue artists' oil color with a small amount of mineral spirits. When the lumps have dissolved, add a little more mineral spirits and an equal quantity of scumble glaze to form a thick, fluid cream. Mix the Prussian blue artists' oil color in the same way. The color should be very dense.

2 Add a few drops of a drier to both glazes.

3 Soak a sponge in water and squeeze out the excess. Smaller pieces of sponge can be used for small objects. Dip the damp sponge in the ultramarine blue glaze and dab it on a plate to spread the glaze.

5 Dab in drifts of the Prussian blue glaze, like a dark river running through the ultramarine blue glaze.

4 Using the sponge, dab patches on the pale ultramarine blue base coat, leaving part of the base coat showing through.

6 Make a bob from cotton-knit fabric wrapped around fiberfill, and secured with a rubber band. Using the bob or a stipple brush, stipple the ultramarine blue area, then the Prussian blue to form cloudy gradations of color. Dab off more color exposing the lighter base color in a few places.

lapis lazuli

9 Soften with a Japanese hake or badger softener to reveal the craters created by the solvent.

7 Soften or polish the surface with a badger brush or Japanese hake, brushing in all directions to create a mirror-smooth finish.

10 To imitate the gold flecks found in lapis lazuli, dip the back of a bristle brush in gold powder and shake off the excess. Tap the brush over the lapis lazuli. The fine spots of gold will stick to the wet glaze.

11 When the lapis lazuli effect is completely dry, varnish with two coats of polyurethane gloss. Thin the first coat with 20% mineral spirits. When dry, smooth any bumps or dust particles with fine sandpaper and apply a second coat of varnish. The high sheen of the varnish gives the impression of polished stone.

8 While the glaze is wet, spatter small areas with a little mineral spirits to dissolve the glaze color and expose the lighter base.

A very dramatic mantelpiece in lapis lazuli and fantasy-pink malachite.

MALACHITE

MALACHITE IS A HIGHLY POLISHED, BRIGHT BLUE-GREEN, SEMI-PRECIOUS STONE. IT GENERALLY OCCURS IN SMALL MASSES RATHER THAN BIG PIECES. LARGER OBJECTS – FOR EXAMPLE, TABLE TOPS – ARE USUALLY MADE FROM OTHER MATERIALS AND VENEERED WITH THIN PLATES OF MALACHITE. THE STRIATIONS IN MALACHITE CAN VARY ENORMOUSLY. FRACTURED WAVY LINES, BANDS OF VARYING WIDTHS AND CONCENTRIC CIRCLES ALTERNATE IN LIGHTER AND DARKER COLORS.

MATERIALS

Phthalo green or monestial green artists' oil color

Raw umber or ivory black artists' oil color

Mineral spirits

Scumble glaze

Gloss polyurethane varnish

Drier

Nylon brush; No. 10

Round sable brush or matchstick

Flat varnish brush

Badger brush or Japanese hake

Mounting board

Cardboard

Cutting knife

Masking tape

Very fine cotton-knit fabric, fiberfill, and rubber band

Ruler

Very fine 'wet-and-dry' sandpaper

2 small dishes

PREPARATION

Base coat
Milky emerald green-colored oil-based paint.

METHOD

1 Cut the mounting board into pieces measuring 4¾" (12 cm) long and different widths: 1", 1½", and 2½" (2.5, 3.8, and 6.5 cm).

2 Mix together phthalo green or monestial green artists' oil color with a little mineral spirits. When the lumps have dissolved add a little more mineral spirits and an equal amount of scumble glaze to form a thick fluid cream. The color should be very dense. For darker areas, prepare another small dish with a mixture of green glaze and a little raw umber or ivory black artists' oil color. Add a few drops of a drier to the paint mixtures.

3 As real malachite does not occur in big pieces, it is usually cut into sections and fitted together to make a large piece. Make a cardboard template of the required size and divide it into angular pieces that fit together like a jigsaw puzzle.

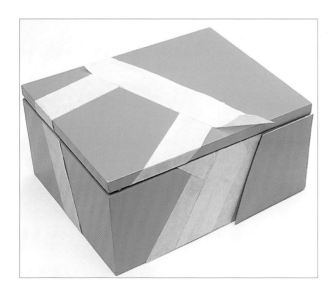

4 Tape around one section of the template with masking tape. Rub down the edges to prevent the paint seeping under the masking tape.

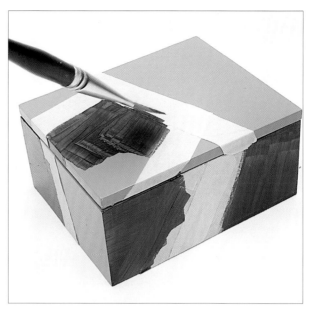

5 Paint green glaze mixture over the base coat with the nylon brush. Paint in darker areas of glaze if desired.

6 Butter the bob with the green glaze mixture. (A 'bob' is made from cotton-knit fabric wrapped around fiber-fill and secured with a rubber band.)

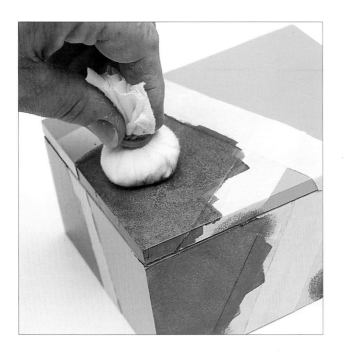

7 Using the cotton bob, dab firmly to remove excess paint and eliminate brush strokes.

9 Take the strips of mounting board and score them with a cutting knife. Do not cut through the board. Pull the board apart, without twisting. Check that the rough, torn edge is relatively straight and that there are no jagged pieces sticking out.

8 Soften or polish the surface with a badger brush or Japanese hake, brushing in all directions.

10 Holding the board almost vertical, use the torn edge to drag off the paint. Start at the top right-hand side of the section, and drag from top to bottom. Make a gradual arc, then stop, push the card at an angle, forming a V-shape, then continue with the curve. The next section should run parallel to the previously painted one.

11 It is advisable to make the nuclei in the form of half-circles at the edge of a section. To achieve this, swivel or pivot the board to make fan-shaped bands.

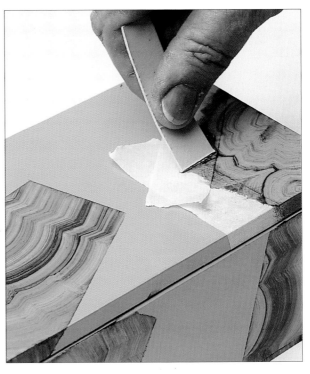

13 Tape around another section, away from the wet area, and repeat the process, varying the pattern.

12 With more card, continue the striations following the pattern until the section is complete.

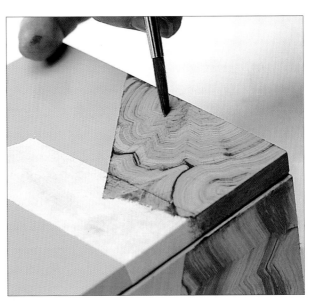

14 Fill in spaces between the striations with a sable brush or a matchstick with a frayed end.

malachite

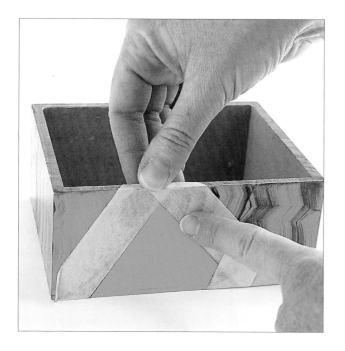

15 Tape around the next section and repeat the process. Remember to rub down the edges to prevent the paint from seeping under the masking tape.

16 Wait for each section to dry before removing the masking tape.

17 When the malachite effect is completely dry, varnish with at least two coats of polyurethane gloss. Thin the first coat with 20% mineral spirits. When completely dry, smooth any bumps or dust particles with fine sandpaper and apply a second coat of varnish. The high sheen of the varnish gives the impression of highly polished stone.

An old, iron bathtub has been given a new and fun look with a malachite paint finish.

MARBLING

THERE ARE MANY WHITE MARBLES, THE PUREST BEING CARRARA, WHICH IS FOUND IN ITALY AND USED FOR SCULPTING. OTHER WHITE MARBLES ARE NOT 'BRIGHT WHITE' AND USUALLY HAVE GRAY, YELLOW OCHRE OR RAW UMBER MARKINGS, WITH DARKER VARIEGATED VEINS. MARBLE CAN BE EXTREMELY SUCCESSFULLY SIMULATED.

MATERIALS

White oil-based paint

Titanium white artists' oil color

Black or Payne's gray artists' oil color

Raw umber, yellow ochre or raw sienna
   artist's oil color (optional)

Mineral spirits

Scumble glaze

Polyurethane gloss varnish or a
   water-based varnish

Brushes; 1" or 2" (2.5 or 5 cm)

Artists' nylon or sable brush; No. 3

Badger brush or Japanese hake

Stippling brush or softener

To make marks (optional):

   Plastic wrap

   Blotting paper

   Flat bristle brush

   Spray bottle, filled with solvent

   Sable brush

   Natural sea sponge

Feather (for veining)

Fine-grade sandpaper

PREPARATION

Base coat

Marbling requires at least two coats of white oil-based paint, that have been finely sanded between coats. The finished surface should be extremely smooth, as natural marble has a highly polished finish.

METHOD

1 Smooth the base coat with fine-grade sandpaper.

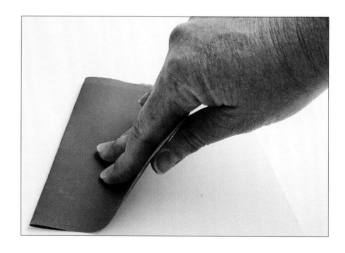

2 Mix together equal quantities of white oil-based paint (or titanium white artists' oil color), mineral spirits and scumble glaze.

3 Create a dark shadow glaze by mixing black or Payne's gray artists' oil color (with a little raw umber if required) and titanium white artists' oil color or white oil-based paint. Dilute the mixture with mineral spirits to form a thin cream. Add an equal amount of scumble glaze for transparency.

4 Draw a plan of the position of the cracks to use as a guide.

5 Using a 1" (2.5 cm) brush, paint the white glaze mixture onto an area measuring about 1 sq ft or 30 sq cm. While the glaze is still wet, add a few pale gray shadows. (Shadows usually run in one direction, but not in parallel streaks.)

6 Stipple the white areas to eliminate brush strokes. Wipe the brush and then stipple to blend the gray areas into the white areas. Darker shadows can be added and blended.

7 Soften the areas with a badger brush.

Markings

A number of techniques can be applied to this surface and immediately softened by brushing in all directions with a badger brush or Japanese hake. Some techniques require different or darker colors to create the full effect.

Plastic wrap

Drop the wrap onto the wet glaze and gently blow on it. As it is lifted, the glaze will pull off, exposing the lighter base coat.

Blotting paper

Crumple the paper and press it onto the glaze, following the line of the darker shadows for a white marble. For a black marble (illustrated here), press the blotting paper onto a black glaze which has been painted over a white-glaze coat. Using mineral spirits and a small brush, accentuate the white lines and soften where required.

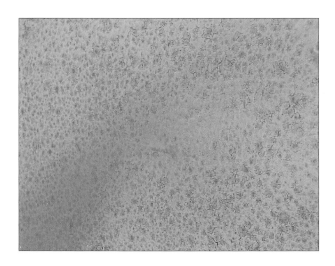

Solvent release 1

Dip a flat bristle brush into mineral spirits and, after flicking off the excess, spatter onto the darker areas. For large flat areas, put mineral spirits into a spray bottle and spray a light mist over the darker areas. This will 'eat away' at the glaze and form craters, exposing the lighter background.

Solvent release 2

Draw a thin sable brush dipped in mineral spirits across the marble to create a pale line or crack. If the crack is softened in only one direction, a darker line will appear where the glaze accumulates.

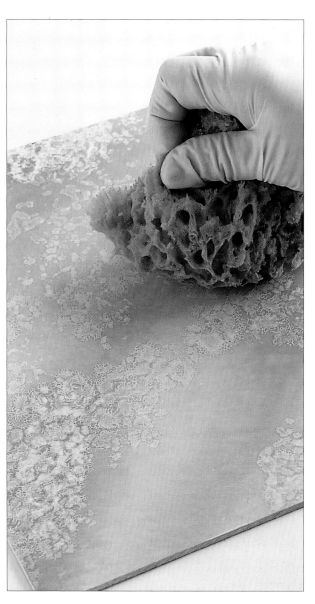

Solvent release 3

Soak a natural sea sponge in water and squeeze it out until it is almost dry. Dip it into a little mineral spirits and pounce lightly on the darker areas to create interesting 'holes'.

Cracks and veining

1 Study the veins in a piece of marble. With a sable brush, paint cracks or striations in the direction of the shadows. Start by painting the veins very pale, then build up the color so that some are thicker and darker; they can disappear into a dark shadow. Soften with a badger brush or Japanese hake.

3 Dip a feather into white oil-based paint, blot off excess paint on a paper towel or a plate.

2 Paint on the next area of glaze, adjoining the wet edge of the completed section, and create more shadows and cracks. Some areas can be left clear – or have fewer marks and cracks – as natural white marble is not heavily veined. Allow the marbling to dry.

4 Roll and pull the feather across the marble. Lift the feather at the end of each stroke and taper the mark. White fractures often run across the gray shadows and cracks.

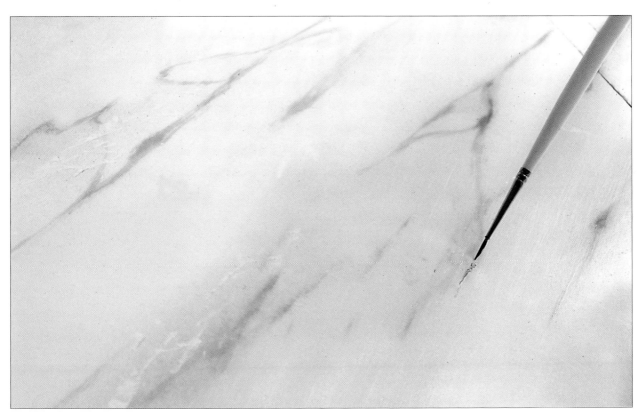

5 A second working of smaller, delicate marks and finer cracks can be done before varnishing. Remember to soften these with a badger brush or Japanese hake.

6 Varnish the marbled item to make it 'polished'. Polyurethane varnish tends to yellow white marbles. Clear water-based varnish can also be used.

Tips
- ✦ A large wall will look more realistic if it is marbled in blocks, leaving a thin line between the blocks.
- ✦ Rag rolling the glaze can create interesting fractures.
- ✦ Crushed newsprint pushed onto the wet glaze leaves an interesting pattern.
- ✦ If the marbling is too dark and the veins are too definite, mix a little white oil-based paint with the varnish (to create a milky varnish) which will soften the effect.

FAUX MARBLE

The same method and materials can be used to create various faux marble effects.

Pink marble

Base coat: White oil-based paint.

Glaze: Alizarin crimson artists' oil color can be mixed with very little ivory black or Payne's gray artists' oil color and equal amounts of scumble glaze and mineral spirits.

Shadows: Raw umber and a bit of yellow ochre artists' oil color mixed with glaze.

Veining: A touch of black added to the artists' oil colors.

Sienna marble

Base coat: White oil-based paint mixed with a little yellow ochre artists' oil color.

Glaze: Raw sienna artists' oil color mixed with equal amounts of scumble glaze and mineral spirits.

Shadows: Burnt sienna or burnt umber artists' oil color mixed with glaze.

Veining: A touch of black mixed with either burnt sienna or burnt umber artists' oil color.

Faux marbling can be used subtly or dramatically on a range of interior features.

SHAGREEN

GENUINE SHAGREEN IS LEATHER THAT HAS BEEN TEXTURED BY PRESSING SMALL SEEDS INTO THE MOIST SURFACE TO CREATE A PITTED EFFECT, AND THEN DYED. IT IS ALSO THE NAME GIVEN TO THE GRANULATED CURED SKINS OF SHARKS AND STING RAYS. THE FINISH OF FINE PITTED CIRCLES IS VERY EFFECTIVE ON SMALL, FLAT OBJECTS, SUCH AS BOXES, AND AS A TABLE-TOP INLAY. TRADITIONALLY, IT IS PALE GRAY–GREEN, BUT IT CAN BE ANY COLOR.

MATERIALS

Sap green artists' oil color

Zinc white artists' oil color

Mineral spirits

Satin polyurethane varnish

Flat nylon brush; 1″ (2.5 cm)

Stippling brush

Badger softener or Japanese hake

Spray mister, filled with water

Fine-grade sandpaper

PREPARATION

Base coat

White oil-based paint that has been tinted with a color.

METHOD

1 For a project the size of a small box, mix together a glaze of 2″ (5 cm) sap green artists' oil color, 1″ (2.5 cm) zinc white artists' oil color and 2 tablespoons (25 ml) of mineral spirits. (These measurements are approximate.) The consistency should resemble thin cream. Add more artists' oil color if the color is not strong enough.

2 Paint the glaze onto the object with a flat nylon brush. If necessary, use a stippling brush to soften any visible brush strokes.

3 Soften the stippled surface with a badger or hake softener to ensure a very smooth painted surface.

4 While the glaze is wet, spray a fine water mist over the surface. As the water droplets evaporate on the oily surface, they will leave the small rings that create the shagreen effect.

5 When the shagreen effect is dry, the object can be varnished. Thin the first coat with 20% mineral spirits. When dry, smooth the surface with fine sandpaper and apply a second coat of varnish.

s h a g r e e n

STONE BLOCKING

THE EFFECT OF DRESSED STONE BLOCKS WITH FINE GROUT LINES WILL ENHANCE ANY FEATURELESS PLASTER WALL, HALL, ENTRANCE OR LOBBY. AN AUTHENTIC-LOOKING TEXTURED STONE EFFECT CAN BE ACHIEVED BY APPLYING WATER-BASED SPACKLE MIXED WITH PAINT. THE BLOCKS CAN HAVE BEVELED EDGES, DOVETAILING WHERE THEY MEET. COLORS SHOULD BE SUBTLE AS NO TWO BLOCKS OF STONE ARE IDENTICAL.

MATERIALS

White water-based paint

Universal stainers: raw umber, raw
   sienna, yellow ochre and black

Raw umber artists' acrylic (optional)

Acrylic scumble glaze

Small can of base color (for
   corrections, if necessary)

Gray/brown water-based crayon

Spackle (optional)

2 or 3 decorators' paintbrushes;
   2" (5 cm)

2 or 3 natural sponges or cloths

Cardboard

Cutting knife

Masking tape; ⅛" (3 mm)

Low-tack masking tape or
   plastic putty

Ruler or straightedge

Carpenter's level

Framing square

Plumb line

Flat spatula

Coarse-grade sandpaper

PREPARATION

Base coat

Two coats of pale ivory-colored water-based paint. The pale base coat will be the color of the grouting.

METHOD

Marking out blocks

1 Measure the height and the width of the wall. Divide the height into blocks, proportional to the size of the room.

2 Cut out a cardboard template for a block. Each block should be twice as long as it is deep.

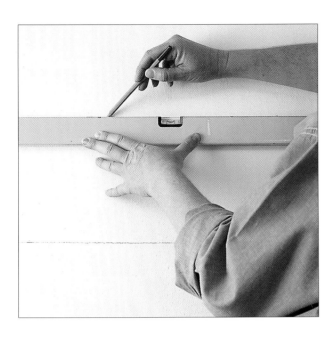

3 Having marked the number of blocks vertically, use the water-based crayon to mark a horizontal line at waist height. Check the position of the horizontal line with a level. (Do not start at the cornice or baseboard as they may not be level.) Mark the horizontal line around the room.

4 Stick the ⅛" (3 mm) tape just above the lines. Continue around the room until all the horizontal lines are in place. Rub down the tape to prevent the paint from seeping underneath it.

5 Mark the center of the wall; using a framing square, draw a vertical line between the horizontal tapes.

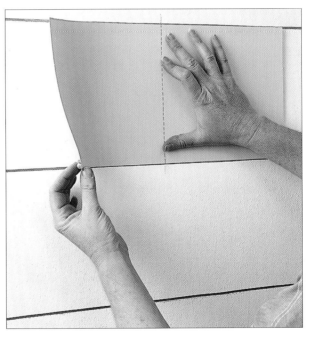

6 Place the cardboard template between the lines in the center of the room. Secure it with low-tack masking tape or plastic putty. This indicates the spacing for the next block.

stone blocking

7 Draw a line from the baseboard to the cornice using the level as a guide, skipping every other block. Drop a plumb line to check that the line is vertical.

8 Place the cardboard template next to the vertical line. Roll the tape from the cornice to the baseboard, but do not rub it down. Continue around the room until all the vertical lines are in place.

9 Cut out alternate vertical tapes to create a block effect. Rub down remaining vertical tapes to prevent the paint from seeping underneath it.

Painting blocks

1 Mix three or four similar tones by adding the universal stainers to white water-based paint. Dilute four parts of each color with five parts water. To increase working time, add about one-third acrylic scumble glaze to the mixture.

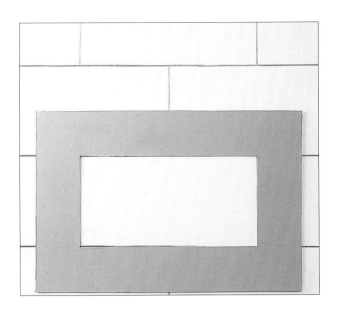

2 Mask off the block you intend working on with pieces of cardboard. Alternatively, fix a big piece of cardboard over the wall with the block cut out of the middle. (The narrow masking tape indicates grout lines.)

4 For a different texture, a flat spatula can be pulled across sections of the spackle. Allow this to dry before painting.

3 For a granular, mortar-like finish, texture can be built up by pouncing spackle onto the block using a damp sponge.

5 The block can be painted by sponging on different colors, brushing, or rubbing with a cloth. Paint up to the edges of the block and then fill in the center.

6 Paint alternate blocks. When these are dry, paint the adjacent blocks. It is best to leave the finish as pale as possible, and darken some areas later.

8 Carefully remove the masking tape. Water-soluble crayon marks can be cleaned with a damp sponge.

7 If you have used spackle, sand the area with coarse-grade sandpaper to reveal the base coat. This will give the wall a stone-grained appearance.

9 If you want the blocks to look more three-dimensional, use diluted raw umber artists' acrylic to shadow them according to the light source. For example, if the light shines from the top left-hand corner, paint a line under and along the right-hand side of the blocks.

Top: The blocking technique on a wall does not have to resemble stone, but can be used creatively in any color.
Above: Classic stone-blocking finish.

TORTOISESHELL

TORTOISESHELL ORIGINATED FROM THE SHELLS OF SEA TURTLES AND WAS VERY POPULAR FOR COMBS AND FOR DECORATIVE INLAYS ON FURNITURE. THE TORTOISESHELL EFFECT IS CREATED FROM VERY LUMINOUS REDS, YELLOWS, ORANGES, GOLDS AND WARM BROWNS. TORTOISESHELL IS ONLY USED AS AN ORNAMENTAL VENEER ON FLAT SURFACES AS IT IS NOT THICK ENOUGH FOR MOLDINGS OR CARVINGS.

MATERIALS

Raw sienna artists' oil color

Burnt sienna artists' oil color

Burnt umber artists' oil color

Mineral spirits

Scumble glaze

Gloss polyurethane varnish

Decorators' flat nylon brush; 1" or 2" (2.5 or 5 cm) (the size of the brush depends on the size of the project)

Japanese hake or badger softener; 2" (5 cm)

Flat short-bristle brush; No. 8 or No. 9

Flat varnish brush

Fine-grade sandpaper

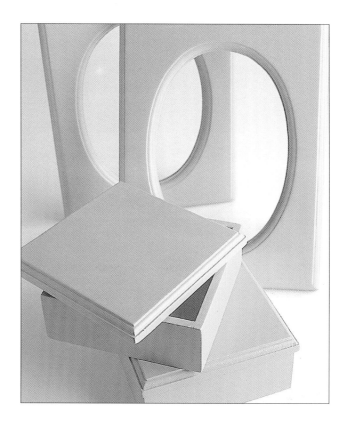

PREPARATION

Base coat

Oil-based paint in a deep, golden straw color, cadmium red, or white oil-based paint stained with raw sienna universal stainer or artists' oil color. If using artists' oil color, mix it well with a little mineral spirits before adding it to the oil-based paint.

Imitation gold metal leaf, also known as Dutch metal, and other imitation leafs are very good backgrounds for a more exotic look.

METHOD

1 Mix together raw sienna artists' oil color (according to the strength of color required) with equal quantities of mineral spirits and scumble glaze, to form a glaze for painting over the base coat.

2 Mix burnt sienna artists' oil color with a little mineral spirits to form a thick cream. This is used for first brush strokes. Mix burnt umber artists' oil color with a little mineral spirits to form a thick cream. This is used for painting 'eyes' in the burnt sienna brush strokes.

3 Brush the raw sienna glaze over the dry base coat. While the glaze is still wet, add the burnt sienna mixture using diagonal brush strokes. Natural tortoiseshell markings are simulated by diagonal brush strokes, usually from the top right-hand corner to the lower left-hand corner. These are often clustered in islands that are quite close together but unevenly spaced.

4 Use the burnt umber mixture and the short-bristle brush to paint 'eyes' on the burnt sienna. (For a paler tortoiseshell, use raw sienna as the first color and burnt sienna for the 'eyes'.)

6 Then soften at right angles and in all directions. The colors will merge and appear cloudy. Tortoiseshell should be very luminous and transparent.

5 Soften the markings with a badger brush or Japanese hake. Soften on the diagonal to lengthen the strokes.

7 When the tortoiseshell effect is completely dry, varnish with polyurethane gloss. Thin the first coat with 20% mineral spirits. When dry, smooth any bumps or dust particles with fine sandpaper and apply a second coat of varnish.

Tortoiseshell can be used effectively on small trinket boxes.

aging and antiquing

IT TAKES CENTURIES OF WEAR-AND-TEAR AND WEATHERING TO

ACQUIRE THE FINISH ON ANTIQUE FURNITURE AND ORIGINAL AGED AND

ANTIQUED WALLS. NOW, WITH THE USE OF PAINT, PAPER, HAMMERS,

CHAINS AND SANDPAPER, AND A BRAVE SPIRIT, YOU CAN RE-CREATE

THESE EXCITING FINISHES. THIS CHAPTER WILL PROVIDE YOU WITH THE

TRICKS OF THE TRADE TO MAKE VIRTUALLY ANYTHING LOOK OLD.

HOWEVER, IT IS IMPORTANT TO LOOK CAREFULLY AT WHERE AND HOW

ITEMS AGE, AND TO APPLY THIS TECHNIQUE TO THE RIGHT PLACES.

Aged walls work well with a combination of old and modern pieces of furniture.

AGED WALL PLASTER

'AGED WALL PLASTER' IS USED TO DESCRIBE OLD PLASTER PAINTED WITH LIMEWASH TINTED WITH EARTH COLORS. THE TECHNIQUE OF SIMULATING OLD WALLS IS VERY POPULAR, WITH THE RETURN OF NATURAL, WATER-BASED MEDIUMS AND COLORS. THE BEST EXAMPLES OF AGED WALLS ARE FOUND IN VENICE AND TUSCANY IN ITALY. HERE, WALLS COLOR-WASHED DECADES AGO HAVE WEATHERED AND MELLOWED; THE COLORS HAVE FADED IN THE SUN, BUT RETAIN THEIR ORIGINAL BRIGHTNESS IN THE SHADOWS OF MOLDINGS AND UNDER LEDGES. THE BRICKWORK MAY BE EXPOSED WHERE PLASTER HAS FALLEN OFF.

MATERIALS

Water-based paint* in any of the following earth colors:

Burnt umber

Burnt sienna

Raw sienna

Yellow ochre

White

Black

or universal stainers added to white water-based paint

Raw umber or black universal stainer (optional)

Artists' acrylic paint (optional)

Acrylic scumble glaze

Paintbrushes; 2" and 5" (5 and 12.5 cm)

Broad Japanese hake

Badger softener

Newsprint

Rolls of brown paper measuring the length of the wall
   (from ceiling to baseboard)

Soft, absorbent cloths/sheeting to make cloths

Coarse-grade sandpaper

PREPARATION

Base coat

Existing or newly painted walls in water-based paint or limewashed walls.

METHOD

1 Mix one or two colors for the base as well as for the darker sections – for example: raw sienna and yellow ochre for yellowed plaster; raw sienna and burnt umber for warmer tones; burnt sienna and burnt umber for stronger tones. These colors can be darkened with a little raw umber or black universal stainer. Dilute the paint mixture with water to the required color.

2 Add one cup of scumble glaze to the paint mixture to make it more transparent and extend working time.

3 Dip the 5" (12.5 cm) brush into the diluted paint mixture and, starting in a corner, paint in a random pattern in a strip about 3 ft or 1 m wide. Alternatively, dip a cloth into the paint and rub it over the wall using a circular motion.

5 When all the walls have been painted, go over them again using a slightly darker color. Corners and areas just below the cornice and above the baseboard should be painted slightly darker. A broad hake can be used to soften the drifted color.

4 As the paint starts to dry, either brush it with a dry brush or rub over it with a dry cloth. Brushing the wet paint in one direction will build up the color and create a water mark or stain.

Faded mural

A soft, faded mural effect can be created by first hand-painting or stenciling a pattern or design using very diluted paint on an already aged wall. Artists' acrylic paint is suitable for this purpose. Once dry, take a piece of fairly coarse sandpaper and sand lightly over the entire mural area to give it a faded and weathered appearance.

'Exposing' plaster or creating a layered lime look

1 When the first coat of paint has dried, brush a piece of torn newsprint onto the wall using a wet brush.

2 Paint the wall with the darker colored paint and then peel off the newsprint to 'expose' the base coat.

A beautifully aged and faded mural transforms this dining room.

3 When you get to the bottom of the wall, peel off the paper. If necessary, soften some areas using a broad hake or badger softener. Continue around the room, painting up to the wet edges of the previous panel and using a fresh length of brown paper for each strip. When the walls are completely dry, sand them to remove bumps and irregularities in the plaster, and to expose the base coat.

Aged plaster (frottage method)

1 Mix the paint mixture with about 25% scumble glaze to extend working time. Paint about a 3 ft or 1 m strip of wall from ceiling to floor.

2 Take a length of brown paper, crumple it, flatten it and then press it onto the wet paint at the top of the wall. 'Smooth' the paper onto the wall using your hand and your forearms in a fanning movement, working from the outer edges of the paper toward the center.

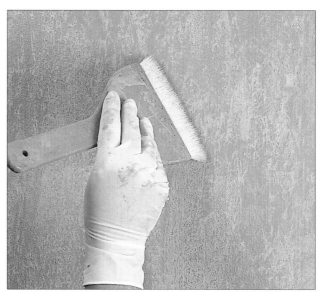

A beautifully textured wall creates the perfect backdrop for exquisite furniture.

AGING AND ANTIQUING

Aging an object will not make it an antique, but objects and furniture can be successfully antiqued to look really old. Genuine antiques accumulate marks and character over the years. Specific techniques can be used to make new pieces appear aged. The 'trick' is to determine how furniture would have been handled: where paint would have worn off; if corners and sharp edges would have been chipped. Aged table tops are often dented or scratched.

Mixture for antiquing glaze

Raw umber artists' oil color (black or burnt umber can be added according to color preference)

Mineral spirits

Scumble glaze

Drier (optional)

A bottle or paint can for storing the mixture

Mix together the artists' oil color and a small quantity of mineral spirits to form a thick cream. Ensure there are no lumps. Add a little scumble glaze for transparency. If the mixture is too dark, add more scumble glaze and mineral spirits. This mixture can be kept in a container. Add a few drops of a drier to speed drying time.

Water-based or oil-based paint (for base coat)

Mineral spirits

Paintbrushes; ¾" (2 cm)

Candle wax

Petroleum jelly (Vaseline®)

Soft cloths

Chain (for making small indentations)

Sharp stone (for gouging and scratching)

Stiff bristle brush/toothbrush

Steel wool

Clear wax/floor polish

Rottenstone

METHOD

NOTE: Items to be antiqued should be new wood or previously painted pieces that have been sanded.

1 Rub candle wax over the areas of 'wear and tear'.

2 Dab or smear petroleum jelly over corners and sharp edges/protrusions where natural chipping would have occurred.

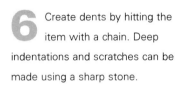

3 Paint on a base coat of water-based or oil-based paint. A wash of diluted paint will create a better effect as the wood or previous coat of paint will show through. An undiluted second layer of paint can be brushed on using a dry brush to create a streaky effect. Brush softly over the petroleum jelly-coated areas.

4 When the paint is dry, wipe off the petroleum jelly to reveal 'chips' in the paintwork.

5 Use a cloth dipped in mineral spirits to remove the candle wax. This exposes the bare wood or base coat, creating 'worn' paintwork.

6 Create dents by hitting the item with a chain. Deep indentations and scratches can be made using a sharp stone.

7 With a cloth, randomly apply the antiquing glaze; a few dabs are quite sufficient. Use a stiff bristle brush/toothbrush to get the glaze into the indentations and carved areas.

8 Spread the glaze using a cloth and allow it to dry for 15 to 30 minutes.

10 A light coat of clear wax – for example, floor polish – will enhance the color and patina.

9 Wipe off the mixture using a dry cloth or steel wool, but leave some of it in the cracks and carvings where dust and dirt would have collected. Lighter areas can be wiped clean with a cloth dipped in mineral spirits.

Spattering spots and stains

Items can be spotted and stained by spattering (*see* page 59).

'Old and dusty'

An old and dusty look can be simulated in grooves or indentations where dust would have collected. Dip a stiff bristle brush into rottenstone or clay powder, shake off the excess, and pounce it onto the antiquing glaze.

This newly crafted cupboard was successfully antiqued to blend in with the aged atmosphere of the room.

VERDIGRIS

WHEN COPPER IS EXPOSED TO THE ELEMENTS, IT TURNS DULL AND THEN BECOMES A BLACKISH GRAY-GREEN. AS IT CONTINUES TO WEATHER, A CHALKY FILM OF PALE TURQUOISE, CALLED VERDIGRIS, BEGINS TO FORM. WHEN IT RAINS, THIS RUNS DOWN THE COPPER IN STREAKS. UNDILUTED HOUSEHOLD BLEACH CAN BE PAINTED ONTO REAL COPPER TO SPEED UP THE PROCESS. IT SHOULD TURN TURQUOISE-BLUE AFTER 24 HOURS, AND IS A GOOD INDICATOR OF THE CORRECT COLOR. IT IS NOT DIFFICULT TO SIMULATE VERDIGRIS; IT IS A FINISH THAT IS USED FREQUENTLY ON WROUGHT-IRON FURNITURE AND ORNAMENTS.

MATERIALS

For water-based finishes (interior use)

Matte black water-based paint

White water-based paint

Turquoise-blue water-based paint

Dark green water-based paint

Raw umber universal stainer

For oil-based finishes (exterior use)

Oil-based equivalents of the
   water-based paints

Mineral spirits

Dry powder pigments (white,
   turquoise, raw umber and black)
   (optional)

Dry spackle powder or rottenstone

Chalk bag, stippling brush or large
   Japanese hake

Brushes; ¾", 1" and 2" (2, 2.5 and
   5 cm)

2 or 3 small natural sea sponges

PREPARATION

NOTE: All wrought-iron furniture and objects must be treated with the correct metal primer.

Base coat

Water-based paint (for interior use) or oil-based paint (for exterior use) in either white, matte black or dark green. Copper and copper leaf may be used.

METHOD

1 Soak the sea sponges in water and squeeze out any excess.

2 Make up basic color mixtures:
- ◆ pale, milky turquoise/green;
- ◆ dark turquoise;
- ◆ putty gray; and
- ◆ dark green;

and 'dirty' them with a little raw umber or black.

3 Paint a base coat of white oil- or water-based paint over the entire surface.

5 Dip a sponge or paintbrush into the dark green paint. Dab off any excess paint and pounce the color onto the object, blending it into the putty gray-colored background.

4 Apply a coat of putty gray-colored paint over the white base coat.

6 While the paint is still wet, dab on the dark turquoise mixture, blending the two colors.

verdigris

7 Use the pale milky turquoise to lighten some areas. Using a dry brush, touch on the raised areas to create highlights.

9 To create a chalky effect, dust spackle powder or rotten-stone (colored, if desired, with pigment powder) sparingly onto the wet paint with a hake, stippler or chalk bag.

8 Spattering can enhance the aged effect.

10 To simulate the rain effect that streaks verdigris, soak a sponge in water or mineral spirits and dribble the solvent down the wet paint. If working in water-based paint, do not seal the verdigris or the chalky effect will be lost.

The verdigris paint finish enhances the classic lines of this decorative urn.

GLOSSARY

Acrylic	Water-based paint that becomes waterproof when dry.
Antiquing	Processes used to simulate natural aging, wear and tear.
Baseboard	A trim, usually wood, between a wall and a floor.
Color washing	Paint technique used to produce a softly textured, patchy finish, achieved by applying several layers of thin paint.
Cornice	The molding between a ceiling and a wall.
Dado	Area of wall below a molded or painted dado rail.
Dado rail	A protective wall rail that originated in the eighteenth century to prevent damage to walls from the backrests of chairs.
Dragging	Technique of pulling a long-haired brush through wet paint or glaze to produce a series of fine lines.
Drier	A medium, or additive, that thins paints and speeds drying time.
Glaze	Transparent or semi-transparent medium (water- or oil-based).
Lapis lazuli	Blue mineral used as a gemstone and as the pigment known as ultramarine blue.
Marbling	Variety of paint techniques designed to re-create artificially the appearance of marble.
Picture rail	Molding running along the top of a wall to take the hooks from which framed pictures hang.
Polyurethane	Synthetic resin used on some paints and varnish.
Ragging	A technique that uses a crumpled rag to create decorative broken color finishes.
Scumble	An oil-based glaze. A water-based glaze is sometimes called an acrylic scumble.
Spattering	A decorative technique in which a brush dipped in paint, glaze or varnish is knocked to spray dots of color onto a surface.
Sponging	A painting technique that uses a damp sponge to create a mottled, patchy effect.
Stippling	A technique used to soften and blend color, to eliminate brush strokes.
Thixotropic	A term used to describe paint that returns to a gel state after mixing.
Trompe l'oeil	Painting that creates an optical illusion or 'deceives the eye'.
TSP	Trisodium phosphate, a concentrated, water-based cleanser that rinses clean without a residue.
Verdigris	The green color produced as a result of naturally occurring corrosion on copper, bronze and brass.

INDEX